Curious
Oxfordshire

Curious Oxfordshire

Roger Long

Artwork by Brenda Allaway
Compilation by Dave Blackman

First published in 2008 by

Reprinted in 2020

The History Press
97 St George's Place,
Cheltenham, Gloucestershire GL50 3QB
www.thehistorypress.co.uk

Copyright © Roger Long, 2008

All rights reserved. No part of this publication may be reproduced, stored in a retrieval system, or transmitted, in any form, or by any means, electronic, mechanical, photocopying, recording or otherwise, without the prior permission of the publisher and copyright holder.

Roger Long has asserted the moral right to be identified as the author of this work.

British Library Cataloguing in Publication Data
A catalogue record for this book is available from the British Library.

ISBN 978 0 7509 4957 6

Typesetting and origination by
The History Press Limited.
Printed by TJ International Limited, Padstow, Cornwall.

Also by Roger Long

A Grim Almanac of Old Berkshire
Historical Inns Along the River Thames

CONTENTS

Author's Note	vii
1. South Oxfordshire	1
2. Central Oxfordshire	49
3. North Oxfordshire	99

AUTHOR'S NOTE

For the last quarter of a century I have written some sixteen books on local counties. They include lesser-known murders, ghosts, pubs and local legends. I am very much afraid that the colourful old pubs and local stories will soon be forgotten with the march of time. Therefore, as with other local writers, the reason for our existence is posterity rather than profit.

The one thing I insist on in all of my books is visiting every site I mention, and there are well over 100 in this book. Obviously I cannot check every week whether or not a pub has been disposed of or an ancient building has been reduced to rubble. To the best of my knowledge though, everywhere I had previously visited still existed when I last checked and the stories, when not heard first-hand, have been attributed to the writers who first brought them to light.

Where this book is concerned, its birth is nearly accidental. It was my intention to study, research and investigate everything strange in Berkshire, Buckinghamshire and Oxfordshire. It was a pleasant if onerous venture. Although I had written several books on all three counties before; facts, legends, customs, fables and strange stories (sometimes a bit questionable) came out of the woodwork. I had told no one of my endeavour and had contacted no publisher, as it was early days.

In 2004 when I was literally snowed under by the material of the three counties, I was thrown a lifeline by Sutton Publishing. They were looking for somebody to contribute to their *Grim Almanac* series; hence, *A Grim Almanac of Old Berkshire* came into being. This led to a radio series on the subject and as I work full-time and write columns in a couple of newspapers, Buckinghamshire and Oxfordshire were put on the back burner.

In mid-2005, I took another look at All That's Strange in Oxon and Bucks. I still had far too many words – over 70,000. I discussed this with the publishers who suggested that I impart my observations to the general public on two more occasions. They also suggested that I changed the titles, thus *Curious Oxfordshire* is ready to meet the public now and *Curious Buckinghamshire* will be sometime in the not too distant future.

Every effort has been made to determine and contact the correct owners of the images in this book. I apologise to if I have inadvertently infringed any existing copyright.

I sincerely hope that readers enjoy this book and it interests them in future publications of mine.

Roger Long
2008

1

SOUTH OXFORDSHIRE

ABINGDON

Joan Foreman in her excellent book *The Mask of Time* tells of the strange experience in Abingdon of three WAAFs during the Second World War.

The three servicewomen, returning from town, had somehow missed their transport back to camp. The night being wet and blustery, they sheltered briefly under a bridge. One of the ladies claims to have experienced some type of *déjà vu* as she was transported back to the days of the thirteenth century's peasant's revolt. She described in graphic detail how she was dressed in rough clothes and was unwillingly carried along by a mass of revolting peasants.

In 1570, Abingdon was the site for the trial of the four famous 'Windsor Witches', Elizabeth Stile (alias Rockingham), Mother Devell, Mother Dutten and Mother Margaret. The four were apprehended at Windsor and arraigned at Abingdon, and then in the county town of Berkshire. Charged with heinous and horrible acts, their conviction was a formality. The four were executed on 26 February 1579. A warlock thought to be in control of the coven was never charged.

At Abingdon, on or around 19 June, the Feast of St Edmund is held and the inhabitants of Ock Street elect the Morris Mayor. After votes have been counted from a wooden ballot box, the Mayor is 'danced in'. The dance starts in Ock Street and then encompasses the main streets of the town before finishing at the site of the celebration supper.

The history of this celebration is said to date from around 1700 and commemorates a battle fought between the occupants of Ock Street and citizens from the rest of the town. The cause of the affray seems unknown but apparently honour was satisfied. In the evening, an ox was roasted and shared between the combatants, the horns of which were mounted on a pole and paraded at the front of the procession.

The Morris Mayor tradition ceased in the late 1880s but was revived shortly before the Second World War.

One of the most colourful characters of the area was Richard Corbet. Corbet was studying divinity at Christchurch, Oxford, but could also be found merrymaking with Ben Jonson and his cohorts in London taverns. Having taken his holy orders, he was installed as the Dean of Christchurch in 1620. Eight years later he became the Bishop of Oxford. Despite his meteoric rise to fame, Corbet never lost his sense of humour or his penchant for a practical joke.

Visiting Abingdon one day, he joined friends for a swift tipple near the Market Cross. While there, he overheard a poor ballad singer bewailing his misfortunes. Apparently nobody appreciated his songs and there were no sales of his sheet music. Corbet was no mean poet and had a fine voice. Taking the poor man aside, he discarded his clerical attire and donned the man's peasant jerkin. It took a matter of minutes to adjust the tunes and lyrics. He then strode to the steps of the Market Cross and sang with gusto for several minutes.

The impression on the crowd was riveting as they listened in silence. As the song ended, the throng thrust forward, eager to obtain the song sheet. Within a matter of minutes, he had sold out. Filling the peddler's purse with coinage, Corbet returned to his ecclesiastic comrades and the tavern's good ale.

Abingdon was also the birthplace and one time home of Wizard Manning. Manning was one of four well-known wizards or 'cunning men' in the Thames Valley. The others were Palmer of Boxford, Coudrey of Crookham Common and Stroud of Tadley.

'Cunning men' were thought to be wise and were often consulted on everything from racehorse chances to weather forecasts. They were also herbal physicians, homespun philosophers and the original private detectives. Manning was also well known in Chipping Norton and Witney. In 1862, he was called to the village of Salford where he sorted out the misdeeds of a local witch. He also performed some type of exorcism at Old Man's Bridge at Faringdon.

While researching *Historic Inns Along the River Thames*, I dropped into the Crown and Thistle. Although the landlord was celebrating the inn's 400th birthday, he still found time to show me around his delightful old pub. As we talked of the colourful history of the house, I posed the inevitable question:

'Have you any resident ghosts?'

'How many do you want?' he asked.

'How many have you got?' I replied.

'Well at least four,' he stated, 'in residence that is, and of course there are a couple that drop in from time to time. These include a strong presence in the bar, a lady who passes through the restaurant, thought to be a waitress, and two haunted bedrooms.'

The uniquely named Broad Face Inn at Abingdon has two macabre explanations for its title. One is that it was called after the bloated faces of drowned bodies, usually suicides, which were drawn from the Thames at the adjacent bridge. The second, an even more macabre explanation, suggests that it was called after the bulbous faces of the people hanged at the nearby gaol. This seems unlikely as

The Crown and Thistle, Abingdon. (Author's collection)

The Broad Face, Abingdon. (Author's collection)

the inn predated the gaol by many years. I would, unfortunately, opt for a less colourful and more mundane explanation: Could it be that the pub faces both the road and the river and has a curved frontage or broad face?

APPLETON

Appleton is the Oxfordshire village associated with strange events in the 1960s. In 1963, some extensive damage was done to the churchyard, the most significant of which was the smashing of several crosses. It is difficult, however, to judge whether there was any ecclesiastical significance to this or if it was just a senseless act of vandalism.

ARDINGTON

Tony Barham in his excellent little book *Witchcraft in the Thames Valley* tells of the fate of Martha Warman. Apparently Martha, a serving girl, was fond of men.

In 1832, accompanied by two male companions, Martha was strolling on a local footpath. An account tells of 'electric fluid' (lightning) striking the three as they ambled along. Poor Martha: 'The bolt passed through the wire of her bonnet and tore her stockings and destroyed her new pair of boots.'

All three were dashed to the ground. The men soon revived but poor Martha died. For years a bench stood at the spot – Martha Warman's seat. It served as a warning to young girls. Mothers and employers would point it out with a warning against promiscuity. 'Look what happened to Martha Warman.'

ASHBURY

A healthy walk away from this attractive village, close to the Ridgeway, stands Wayland's Smithy.

Firstly the facts about this very famous location. Wayland's Smithy is an impressive Neolithic tomb or long barrow dating from 3700–3400 BC. Long barrows usually consisted of an inner wooden lining paved with stone in which the bodies of ancient dignitaries were enclosed. Then the structure was covered by a massive earthen mound, which, in the case of Wayland's Smithy, is some 200ft long. A small cross-shaped stone was then placed at one end to denote the entrance and six large flat stones were placed in pairs at the other.

When the tomb was excavated in 1919, eight skeletons were unearthed along with a quantity of short iron bars, the latter in no small way imitating the legend of

Wayland's Smithy. Much restoration work was done in the 1960s with the result of the barrow becoming a bit of a showpiece.

The legend concerning Wayland's ghost is colourful to the extreme, if indeed a little implausible. According to ancient legend, Wayland, a popular smith and metalworker, was imprisoned by Nithuthr, the hated Swedish king. He was tortured and maimed to such a degree that his body was deformed and his face horrendously disfigured. However, while in captivity, Wayland was able to construct a pair of wings from a very light metal and made good his escape. In revenge, Nithuthr tempted the king's two sons with a treasure chest – slamming the lid shut and snapping their necks when they peered inside. He then raped the king's young daughter, sending her back pregnant to her father. Having wreaked his terrible revenge upon Nithuthr, Wayland flew to Berkshire, where he erected his smithy. Being shy of his awful appearance, Wayland would not meet his customers, the merchants who travelled the ancient Ridgeway path. Therefore, the story arose that horses that had thrown a shoe were left outside the smithy at night and then collected newly shod the following morning, silver bars being left in payment for the cautious smith's collection.

Legend grew and fed upon itself, as legends do. Wayland became part of mythology and his shyness led people to think of him as invisible. Sir Walter Scott mentions him in *Kenilworth*.

An equally unlikely postscript is that Norsemen finally discovered Wayland's whereabouts and lay in wait for him. When the mighty smithy returned, he set about them with his hammer, killing eight of them (the excavated skeletons) but received a fatal sword blow himself. Wayland died alone on the Berkshire Downs; his body was never discovered but his benign ghost still shods horses for silver bars.

Wayland's Smithy, Ashbury. (Author's collection)

ASSENDON

The body of Laura Dungey, a young spinster, was found at Lambridge Wood Farm in December 1893. She had been brutally beaten to death. A wealthy London businessman by the name of Mash owned Lambridge Wood Farm; however, very little farming went on there. It is alleged that 23-year-old Laura was conveniently lodged there for Mash's enjoyment while he and his family lived in a house at nearby Henley.

Laura's body was discovered by two young boys, the Froome brothers. The police were called and the tiny village was soon humming with specialists, while the papers had a field day. Suspicion soon fell on one Walter Rathall who lodged with his family at the nearby Red Lion public house. Having been identified by several witnesses as having been in the location on or about the time of the murder, Rathall lived in dread of constables knocking on the door. After hearing nothing for two days, Rathall grabbed his wife and infant and took to the hills. Police Superintendent Francis Keal of Oxford was in charge of the case. He had the greatest suspicion of Rathall and now, working on the premise that innocent men don't run, he organised a search. Rathall's description was sent all over the country and a £100 reward was offered.

Three weeks later Rathall was arrested in Daventry. On 12 January, he appeared before a magisterial enquiry where the alibi that Walter Rathall had concocted was torn to shreds by the prosecution. However, his lawyer, Mr Woods, famous for his verbal dexterity, managed to muddy the water to a surprising degree and Walter Rathall walked from court a free man.

The court may have cleared Rathall of murder but it did little for marital harmony in the area. George Dawson, a relative of Walter, gave evidence describing a scene where Mrs Mash had set about Laura Dungey with an umbrella after accusing her of infidelity with her husband. It also came to light that Walter Rathall, described as a very good-looking man, often paid visits to Lambridge Wood Farm when Mash was in London.

No one was ever charged with the heinous murder of Laura Dungey. However, there was a rumour at the time that George Dawson had tried it on with Laura, but lacking both Mash's affluence and Rathall's fair features, he was shown the door. Dawson, a foreman for Mash, was sacked the following morning. Reputedly Dawson was a tempestuous and violent man.

BIX

Some slight distance from Bix village, the lonely ruins of an ancient church can be found. The Church of St James seems remote and overgrown, while even the air seems laden with the occult and supernatural.

In 1925, interested parties decided that this was a pagan site, with ley lines connecting West Wycombe, an earthwork at Chesham and Berkhamstead Castle. This is also an area notorious for sightings of flying saucers and a major junction for pilgrims to Glastonbury. Tony Barham's *Witchcraft in the Thames Valley* is most informative about this area, telling us that a film was made here containing witchcraft sequences, much against the wishes of the local populace.

BLEWBURY

Henry VIII owned a hunting lodge here named Hall Barn which became the home of a local family named Fuller during the Civil War. During restoration work in the twentieth century, a wall was removed from the lodge and a document was discovered, a paper declaring John Fuller's allegiance to Cromwell, Fuller having been forced to entertain both sides during the war. Who knows, perhaps the gentleman was a born survivor and hidden somewhere there is a similar proclamation showing his support of the Royalists.

One of the most famous characters in the area was the curate, Revd Morgan Jones, known as the 'Blewbury Miser' from Llandovey in Wales. He arrived in 1781 and remained until 1824. During that time he managed to keep his spending down to 2s 6d per year.

The ruins of the Church of St James, Bix. (Author's collection)

The Blewbury Miser would make rounds, dining with his parishioners, receiving a breakfast here and a lunch there. He would then sit by a nearby hearth warming himself. When sufficiently heated, he would rush home before feeling the cold, and once home, he would wrap himself in his one and only patched coat until morning. Morgan Jones managed to live for over forty years without touching his stipend of £50 per year or the £30 rent he received from two small cottages he had inherited.

It was once stated that the miserly reverend heard that a farmer had placed an old suit on a scarecrow. Morgan was up early the following day to walk the five mile round trip to the farm. Once there, he removed the scarecrow's hat which had a better brim than his own and on returning home, he substituted the new brim for the old.

The country reverend's fame spread far and near, to the extent that Charles Dickens modelled Blackberry Jones in *Our Mutual Friend* upon him.

At the age of 80, Morgan Jones intended to retire to Wales but relatives who came to see the old man took note of his ragged state and made excuses that the trip would be too much of an ordeal for him. But a hint from a local suggested that the old gentleman was far more affluent than his ragged attire might suggest and so Morgan Jones travelled to Llandovey with his unenthusiastic relatives. They were soon to be rewarded; Jones died a short time later leaving £18,000 – an astronomical amount of money in those days.

Another Blewbury character was the old landlord of the Blueberry Inn, Malachi Grace. In the nineteenth century, Malachi supported his inn by working part-time as a carter, conveying goods to Reading and Newbury. Grace was fond of his tipple and on many occasions his horse was left to find its own way home, with Malachi lying in a stupor in the back.

One evening some local jokers found him in this condition with his horse munching the roadside grass. Freeing the horse, the pranksters pushed the cart and its occupant into a nearby barn. On awakening, Malachi was quoted making the following speech: 'Be I Malachi Grace? Be I Malachi Grace? If I be, I've lost a horse and if I aint, I've found a cart.'

On leaving Blewbury in the direction of Reading, one would have once come across 'The Man with a Load of Mischief'. This inn sign is not as unusual as one might think; similar signs are based on a picture by Hogarth. The main picture shows a man with a hefty wife on his shoulders. She has a bottle in her hand and is obviously the worse for drink. The poor man also carries a magpie and a monkey in his arms, probably representing theft and stress. A chain often seen around the man's neck represents debt. Not a happy man.

The Blueberry Inn, once the New Inn, the King William and then its current name, stands at the western end of the village. During coaching days, several guests mysteriously disappeared here after spending the night. Legend dictates

The Blueberry Inn, Blewbury. (Author's collection)

that they were murdered and buried in the back garden, and a fruit tree was placed on each independent grave.

Nothing was ever proven against the landlord of the Blueberry Inn and strangely enough, it is neither he nor any of his unfortunate victims that supposedly haunt the premises.

Instead it is a far more recent owner, a man named Edwin who died in 1951. (I shall refrain from using the gentleman's surname as he may still have relatives in the area. When we did a recent BBC broadcast from the inn, we were asked to show the greatest respect.) Suffice it to say, the hollow footsteps sometimes heard late at night passing from a bedroom to the bar are suspected to be those of the ex-landlord.

BRIGHTWELL-CUM-SOTWELL

Brightwell-cum-Sotwell has a gruesome story indeed. During the reign of Henry VIII, pockets of the county were not covered by the King's Writ (which was issued by way of a commandment and was upheld by localised courts). At Brightwell, a priest was struck down and murdered at the altar. The murderer fled across the Thames at Clifton Hampden, thereby escaping to the Chilterns, which were not covered by the Royal Writ.

CHECKENDON

The ghosts of Checkendon Court are four grey nuns who walk in single file between the yew trees. Witnesses state that the cowled figures glide slowly along, their heads bent as if in prayer. Tony Barham, in *Witchcraft in the Thames Valley*, informs us of a Polish family who witnessed the phantom nuns just after the Second World War. The family were one of many evacuated to the area. As they were new arrivals and spoke very limited English, it is doubtful that the authentic details of their story had been influenced by knowledge of any local legend.

Checkendon Church was planned to be built on an old quarry surrounded by yew trees, still referred to as the Devil's Churchyard. Each morning the builders found their masonry had been moved to another site. Some say that the villagers had decided on re-siting the church away from the unhallowed ground; others are convinced that the Devil wanted no encroachment on his ground.

Nearby, the 'Watch Folly Tree' was always given a wide berth by tramps and itinerant workers. The old tree traditionally marks the spot where a shepherd boy hid to watch thieves rustling his flock. He was discovered, dragged from the branches and murdered. The story goes that wanderers sleeping beneath the tree experience nightmare re-enactments of the murder. In the seventeenth century, Watch Folly was thought to be a meeting place for witches, but there is no valid evidence of this.

CHILDREY, NEAR WANTAGE

Childrey is situated on the B4507 and in September 1986, an unusual crop circle was discovered here. The symmetry of the circle is extremely accurate and the pattern is most complicated. Crop circles, if inexplicable, are not uncommon.

The story arises when an expert in this field (no pun intended) took home a soil sample from the site, whereby all sorts of burglar alarms went off and several clocks stopped. A more complete report on the above may be found in *Circular Evidence* by Pat Delgadd and Colin Andrews.

CHRISTMAS COMMON

Close to Watlington is a very small hamlet called Christmas Common. A local view suggests that Christmas Common got its name during the Civil War as the centre of a battlefield where a cease-fire was called on Christmas Day to observe the birth of Christ.

Four nuns walk in ghostly style at Checkendon Court, Checkendon. (Author's collection)

The 'Watch Folly Tree' at Checkendon. (B. Allaway)

Another disappearing grey horse, this time with a rider, is reputed to haunt Christmas Common. There have been several sightings over the years including one where a driver mentally noted the details. The horse, as stated, was grey and the rider, whose gender was unknown, had long hair and wore a brown jacket. There was snow on the ground at the time but the ghostly pair left no prints.

CLIFTON HAMPDEN

The Plough Inn at Clifton Hampden has an abundance of quite well substantiated ghosts. The most active of these is an unseen spirit that is adverse to alcohol. In 1966, an invisible hand picked up the landlady's drink and tipped it upside down, dashing the contents to the floor. The spiritual abstainer has repeated the procedure on several occasions since.

Silent apparitions frequent the Plough and are well attested to by the locals. There is also a blue light that floods the bar and the sound of a door opening where there isn't one.

The Plough also possesses what we in the trade call a 'nudger'. These playful manifestations are generally supposed to be the earthbound spirits of dogs; they are never seen but often felt. One experiences a sharp jar or nudge in the behind while having a drink or conversation. This action is interpreted as coming from a spectral canine, who, like his living counterparts, is suffering from a lack of attention.

Yet another spirit at the Plough is thought to be John Hampden. Hampden was a cousin to Oliver Cromwell and is often blamed for initiating the chain of events that led to the Civil War. If Hampden was to blame, it did him little good; he was one of the first casualties. He died in an early battle, a victim of Prince Rupert's cavalry. This much-maligned historical character was a regular at the Plough and it is rumoured that his pensive spirit still treads the ancient boards there.

The sad story of Courtiers, a square-faced Georgian building at Clifton Hampden, is recounted in a charity booklet produced by the Abbey Monastery Guest House. The sombre story relates to the sad case of Sara Fletcher. Sara was the infatuated wife of one Captain Fletcher, RN. Fletcher was a charming but promiscuous man who was a devil for the women. Sara forgave him several indiscretions but when she interrupted Fletcher's bigamous marriage ceremony at Courtiers, she could take no more.

Fletcher ran back to sea and Sara returned to her bedroom and, sadly, hanged herself. The date was 7 June 1769; the victim, an attractive loyal young woman of 29.

A ghostly hand may relieve you of your pint at the Plough at Clifton Hampden. (Author's collection)

The Plough also has a phantom nudger. (B. Allaway)

For the days of secretive austerity, we are given quite a graphic description of the suicide. Sara hanged herself from the curtain rail of her four-poster bed using a handkerchief and a piece of cord. She was wearing a black silk cloak and sported a purple ribbon in her auburn hair. Sara's ghost, thus attired, frequents the grounds and house of Courtiers. The face, though lovely, is fraught with anguish, as the restless spirit makes its way to the bedroom where she died.

Romantic legend dictates that over the years, some young men who have witnessed the apparition have fallen instantly in love with her. There is even a story that her beautiful spirit entered the dreams of a young landscape gardener in far away Bournemouth.

What is surprising is that the narrow-minded regime of the late eighteenth century permitted Sara to be buried in consecrated grounds. Sara is interred at Dorchester Abbey. Her tombstone is even more absolving. It recounts a lady of 'blameless innocence' who was 'unable to cope' and was 'a martyr to excessive sensibility'.

CROWELL

Most of Crowell was burnt down in 1759. The Catherine Wheel public house is a strong claimant to being the first building to rise, phoenix like, from the ashes. When I visited the inn, I was impressed by a copy of the chair used by John Bunyan in Bedford Gaol. Bunyan regularly played the flute while incarcerated, but searches by the warden could never discover the whereabouts of the instrument. The answer was that the flute had been cleverly designed as part of the chair's structure.

In the 1960s, John Camp described in his fascinating book *Oxfordshire and Buckinghamshire Pubs* how the eccentric landlord had removed two bricks from his convenience, thus giving a convenient view of the graveyard opposite. One of Camp's suggestions is that it was a tactful reminder that time flies and that it might be an idea to get another drink in before 'The Last Trumpet Calls'.

CROWMARSH GIFFORD

Mr Barham informs us that Crowmarsh Gifford once possessed a witch named Minty Frewin. As everybody knows, witches are inquisitive, and show an interest in their neighbours' welfare.

Minty had a unique way of keeping up with the local gossip; she had trained a mouse hawk (short eared owl) to fly around the district and report conversations to her. The idea had one flaw, the bird, being well feathered, suffered greatly from the heat and refused to go on duty on warm evenings. This annoyed Minty but the bird would not budge, so she took the desperate measure of turning herself into a white cat and went prowling around the village gathering information. How successful she was is not known.

DIDCOT

There is a rather nice little story here of a Didcot man who somewhat overdid the celebrations the night before his wedding. During the evening of drunken revelry, he took a large hammer into the local church and smashed a holy water stoup (basin). He was forgiven by the authorities and his marriage was 'blessed' with eleven children, every one of them a girl.

DORCHESTER

Aerial photographs near Dorchester have revealed a complicated series of monuments, including a set of two parallel lines deep in the earth and a nearby cursus. Further exploration showed that the traces of three monuments featured pits or rings with cremations either encircled by them or nearby. However, pits dug in other circles showed no functional purpose. It has been suggested that the seemingly non-functional pits were used to store water.

There is, however, another school of thought which believes that the empty pits, which pre-date 2500 BC, were used in conjunction with the nearby cremation pits for some unknown religious purpose.

Dorchester was a large and impressive town some 1,000 years ago. It was the capital of Mercia and boasted a cathedral, a monastery, an abbey, an abundance of churches and a plethora of inns.

As the town waned in importance, buildings fell into disrepair and were finally demolished. The abbey still remains, however, and thankfully so do several of its old inns.

The George, dating from about 1140, is one such example and as an intriguing old inn as one would care to sup at. To my shame, I did not know that there is a bricked-up tunnel here that once led to the abbey. I discovered this when doing yet another BBC programme here and a delightful young manageress showed me around the cellar. With the abbey being just a stone's throw away and the George being its hospice at one time makes this supposed connecting passage more believable than most.

The George's one ghost has nothing to do with the cellar, which would seem to be its logical habitat. The White Lady appears in the strangely named Vicar's Room. She appears beside the four-poster bed and is described as mournful. The cause of the lady's grief is unknown and her extremely brief appearance makes it impossible to ascertain. The lady just manifests herself, turns briefly, and then disappears.

EAST HENDRED

A resident of East Hendred was once startled to see a troop of phantom soldiers tramping through his house. Apart from the initial shock, the witness's secondary surprise was that the troops had no feet. Later investigation proved the troopers to be Roundheads, a fact suggested by the owner's description of their attire. History relates that after the Battle of Newbury, Cromwellian troops were stationed at the house. Since that time, the building has gone through some internal alterations, one of these being the raising of the floor by about a foot. Could this explain the missing feet?

One of the finest views of delightful East Hendred is from the unusual thirteenth-century Champs Chapel. It was built in grey ashlar by the Carthusians and is now a museum.

The church has an invisible clock which you can hear trotting out the hours. It has been a feature of the village since 1525 and is one of England's oldest timepieces, chiming the quarters and hours and playing the occasional hymn. What makes the clock unique is that it has no faces, hence the invisible clock.

EWELME

Buried in Ewelme Church is Dame Alice Chaucer, granddaughter of author Geoffrey and wife of William de le Pole, Duke of Suffolk. The tomb has three layers. On top is Alice's effigy, decorated with a ducal coronet, on her forearm is the Order of the Garter and, I quote, 'a mouth like a public school matron'. A box at the middle level contains her remains. The bottom layer, which can only be appreciated by lying on one's stomach, is a hideous stone sculpture of the duchess in her death throws. In the churchyard is the grave of Jerome K. Jerome, author of *Three Men in a Boat*.

Ewelme has what is claimed to be a sacred lake, which in actuality is little more than a village pond. There is some sort of legend here, which even the locals fail to remember.

Ewelme Church, containing the tomb of Dame Alice Chaucer. (Author's collection)

Dame Alice Chaucer in her death throes. (B. Allaway)

Ewelme's eerie lake. (Author's collection)

FARINGDON

The folly constructed by Trenwith Wills and Lord Gerald Wellesley, later the 7th Duke of Wellington, was commissioned by the 14th Lord Berners and is the most recently validated folly in Britain. In 1935, Lord Berners had a lot of trouble from local dignitaries when he made known his intention of building a 140ft tower on a hill outside the town. Berners won the day but not before the papers had had a great deal of fun describing the folly as 'Lord Berner's monstrous erection'.

Tony Barham in his *Witchcraft in the Thames Valley*, tells the story of Warlock Manning, a respected cunning man, and Old Man's Bridle, a wooden structure that crossed the Thames just north of Faringdon. Apparently in Victorian times, a malicious gossip was slandering the village. Not wanting the expense of a lengthy court case, the locals contacted Manning who listened to the complaints and then insisted that small slabs of pine were cut and the names of all concerned were written upon them. They were then to be taken to the Thames at midnight and thrown into the river. As the small slices were swept away, so was the gossip and scandal of the village.

There is more than a little confusion in identifying the spectre that walks the graveyard at Faringdon church. To complicate matters, the apparition is headless. It is said to be dressed in clothes of the seventeenth century as it perambulates the north wall of the church adjoining Faringdon House. On enquiry, one will be told that the ghost is one of the Uncton family (Christian name unknown), who was beheaded after the Civil War. He defended Faringdon House, or possibly Wadley Hall, a mile to the east. One can perm either of the above mentioned venues with the names of Robert Pye Senior or Junior. Both are candidates for the headless haunter.

During the Civil War, Robert Pye Senior, a Royalist, defended Wadley Hall (or Faringdon House) against his son, Robert Pye Junior, a Parliamentarian. Let us assume for expediency's sake that it was Faringdon House, as it is much nearer the ghostly promenade, and also fell victim to a battle of the Civil War when an intended cannonball took away the spire of the adjacent church. Robert Pye Senior withstood his son's siege but died a disillusioned man. Robert Pye Junior died of old age in 1701, and this semi-demolished house was not restored until 1780.

Neither Pye Senior nor Junior seem to be a fitting subject for a headless ghost. However, there is one more candidate for the spectre, another Pye; Hampden, grandson of Robert Junior.

Hampden Pye has been immortalised by R.H. Barham in his *Ingoldsby Legends*, appearing as Hamilton Tiche. In real life, Hampden Pye became an admiral but the story is that his jealous stepmother bribed one of his captains to blow his head off during an encounter with the French. The plot was successful; the admiral's death appeared to be an accident. Suspicion was rife but facts were few.

Headless Admiral Hampden Pye was then reputed to haunt the old church and family home at Faringdon, as well as his stepmother's carriage, in which he would suddenly appear beside her. The spectre also haunted the scheming captain's house and often tapped the shoulder of the gunner that fired the fatal shot. Quite a busy schedule for a spirit with an identity crisis – enough to send someone off his head (or vice versa).

There seems to be little doubt as to the identity of the poltergeist that haunted Oriel Cottage at Faringdon. It is presumed to be an ex-tenant who committed suicide at the old building in Wicklesham Road. Some sort of activity had been experienced here for eighteen years, the poltergeist actions becoming more intense rather than abating. The Oriel Cottage ghost brought with it such an extreme drop in temperature and such an atmosphere of powerful malevolence that the family found it impossible to stay in the building. The fear and dread was such that the children refused to venture upstairs at any time of the day or night.

Actions were taken: Builder's reports were made on the structure. Two policemen stayed the night and were greatly unnerved by inexplicable sounds. Mediums were called in. The haunting, however, remained and intensified, culminating in a terrifying shapeless entity manifesting itself before some twenty witnesses. Shortly after one of several exorcisms in 1964, the spiritual activity ceased as abruptly as it had begun.

Lord Berner's folly, Faringdon. (Author's collection)

GORING

Goring was witness to a terrible disaster in 1674. Before the bridge was built in the 1830s, the only way across the Thames was by ferryboat. After a large winter feast day, there were over a hundred people on board, far above the small boat's capacity as it attempted the crossing from Goring to Streatley on the opposite bank. Reports in the London and Oxford papers accused the ferryman of 'imprudently rowing too near the lock'.

Reports on the accident are scarce but one account states that the ferryboat tried too late to pull away, and overturned, tipping its passengers into a freezing river. Between fifty and sixty men, women and children drowned. Blame was thrust from one village to the other. Streatley blamed the Goring ferryman while Goring blamed a host of Streatley passengers that jumped on at the last minute. The disaster caused a deep rift between the two villages for over a century.

The above disaster must have been witnessed from the strangely named Miller of Mansfield on Goring's side of the river, an inn which has been here since the thirteenth century. The story goes that a miller, presumably from Mansfield, offered to sell poached royal venison to a stranger. When the stranger revealed himself as King Henry II, and with poaching being a capital offence, the miller begged for his life. The King offered a royal pardon if the miller agreed to open an inn on the spot, which he subsequently did.

The story may just have a grain of truth in it. Henry's mistress was Fair Rosamund whom he had installed at Godstow. Goring was in a very bleak county in those days and about midway between Windsor and the Fair Rosamund. What a handy place for an inn, especially one run by a man who would trust you with his life.

GROVE

I am indebted to Joan Foreman for a little haunting story concerning a disused aerodrome at Grove. While gathering material for a book, Joan received a letter from a gentleman who had worked at the airfield. At the time (1969), the buildings were being used as a sterilisation plant for the Atomic Energy Authority. The correspondent stated that he was in one of the transformed hangars one night when he heard a rumbling of voices, the sort of sound obtained when a group of people chat together. The sound is audible but individual expressions are lost. The gentleman investigated but found nothing. The same man experienced a similar uncanny conversation on several occasions, but having reported the original episode and having been slightly ridiculed, he remained taciturn about the other incidents.

After several weeks, the man was approached by a colleague who had experienced similar phenomena in the same converted hangar. This at least added credibility to the original story. As with most ghost stories, there is no satisfactory conclusion. At some later stage, the hauntings were such that a psychic research organisation was brought in. The outcome of their investigations is unknown. Finally, the correspondent mentioned that he had discovered that an American airman had hanged himself in the hangar during the war, though this may or may not have had anything to do with the haunting.

HENLEY

Henley is one of many places on the River Thames where 'swan upping' takes place. In the third week of July, the swans are divided between the Queen and two of the oldest London guilds – the Dyers and the Vintners. The brightly dressed swan masters and their assistants mark every swan – not an easy job in a rickety boat with a large outraged cob. The cygnets belonging to the two guilds are given nicks on their beaks: two for the Vintners and one for the Dyers; while the Queen's birds are left unmarked but recorded.

Incidentally, several pubs along this part of the river were named the Swan With Two Necks, obviously a corruption of the 'swan with two nicks'.

Slightly behind Henley Town Hall stands the magnificent Friar Park. This French Gothic mansion was once the home of Beatle George Harrison and is still very private.

Friar Park was built in 1896 for a wealthy local solicitor, Sir Frank Crisp by his architect, M. Clark Edwards. Crisp spared no expense as he let his imagination run wild, both in the house and in the park. There are grandiose caves such as the Large Cave, the Skeleton Cave, the Wishing Well Cave, the Gnome Cave and the Illusion Cave; all are lit by tasteful electric light and are approachable by boat, as indeed are the romantic Blue Grotto, Ice Grotto and Vine Grotto.

Occasionally, Sir Frank's sense of humour wore a little thin with his friends. In Victorian times, electricity was very much a novelty so electrically motivated crocodiles, monkeys and skeletons jumping out from the shadows would have been almost unique and far scarier than in the present day.

I've never entered Friar Park but hope it will be open to the public one day.

Like other towns, Henley has had a tradition of witchcraft over the centuries. According to legend, there seems to have been feline related mysticism in the town for nearly 300 years. In the early eighteenth century, a strange cult was discovered baptising a cat. Even stranger, two centuries later, the Revd Robert Mason, who lived near Henley church, seems to have delved very deeply into the occult. Later in life, the affluent Mason turned recluse, and seldom left his house.

At his death in 1841, Mason was discovered with a Rosicrucian lamp, a collection of mummified cats and a rare cellar of tent wine. He also left £70,000, which, if my maths is correct, is the equivalent to £2 million at today's value.

There is also a story of a strange brass figure found in a Henley pond. It is thought to be connected with the Revd Mason, but if so, it is a very tenuous association indeed.

Prophecies abound with gypsy people; which I can attest to, having been deeply associated with them for years. A story tells of Urania Boswell who, between 1880 and 1920, foretold that men would fly, and is even thought to have forecast submarines. It is said that she warned the American businessman Vanderbilt not to take the maiden voyage of RMS *Titanic* in 1912. He ignored her warning and was subsequently drowned.

Most of the hauntings of Henley are synonymous with or revolve around Mary Blandy. In the mid-eighteenth century, Mary Blandy was a spinster of the town who lived in a large house in Hart Street with her father. Mary, feeling she was past her prime, was more than flattered by the attentions of a young soldier named Cranstoun and they were soon planning their nuptials. Her father, however,

Henley Church and buildings. (Author's collection)

Oxford Castle, Henley. (Frith)

objected to the marriage, considering the man to be a fortune seeker. Mary decided to poison her father and her lover prudently absconded to the Continent. Mary was arrested; she made a half-hearted attempt at escape from house arrest but was soon recaptured and transferred to Oxford Gaol, where she was interred and finally hanged in 1752. Many locals believed her innocence, more out of a sense of regional loyalty than any serious consideration of the facts.

The shade of a mournful young woman that supposedly haunts Blandy House in Hart Street can be no other than the ex-mistress, Mary Blandy. The spectre stands meekly near an old mulberry tree. Occasionally she is accompanied by her lover, Captain Cranstoun, who seems to be more constant in death than he was in life.

A play by Joan Morgan called *The Hanging Wood* tells of the life, romance and death of Mary Blandy and paints a rather rose-tinted picture of the heroine. When the play was performed at the Kenton Theatre at Henley in 1969, all manner of supernatural events took place. Doors slammed in people's faces, lights turned off and on of their own accord, a mirror jumped off of the wall, a cup leapt off of a table and a shadowy figure of a young lady appeared just off stage. Make what you will of these reports.

A Henley haunting that has nothing whatsoever to do with Mary Blandy occurs in the town centre. The charismatic and ancient Bull Inn has a vague reputation for an obscure supernatural activity. The aroma of burning candles is sometimes detected and, less frequently, a cowled figure appears in one of the bedrooms.

Mary Blandy, bewtiched by Captain Cranstoun. (British Museum)

The Bull Inn, Henley. (Author's collection)

HINTON WALDRIST

Hinton Manor is protected by a moat which was once part of the defences of a medieval castle. The manor started life in the Elizabethan period but was added to in 1700. However, much of the building was greatly renovated in 1830. Hinton Manor has one of the many floating lady ghosts reported throughout the country. This one is slightly unusual, being a Red Lady, or to be more precise, a lady in red. The manifestation appears in the music room where she sits with an old-fashioned spinet. The long wine red or maroon dress, thought to be of Elizabethan origin, rustles as she stands. She then smiles benignly before vanishing.

There is a story at Hinton Manor, possibly true, about a lady houseguest back in the 1930s. The guest was wandering the premises prior to a cocktail party and later dinner when she heard the haunting strains of a spinet coming from the music room. On investigation, saw the phantom lady in her long attire. She closed the door so as not to disturb her and on returning to her husband, scolded him for not telling her it was formal dress. It was several minutes before she could be made to comprehend that she had witnessed Hinton Manor's ghostly Red Lady.

Hinton Manor, Hinton Waldrist. (Author's collection)

IDSTONE

The Old Berkshire Village Book, a worthy volume with contributions from Berkshire's Women's Institutes, informs me that there was once a pub in Idstone named Trip the Daisy. Trip was a notable coursing hound whose master kept the local hostelry and honoured it with his name. Now a private abode, it is possible that it still contains an old painting of Trip accompanied by the following rhyme:

> A dog am I, as you may see,
> There can no harm be found in me,
> My master, he confines me here,
> To tell you that he sells good beer.

KINGSTON LISLE

Kingston Lisle is one of the charming villages that Oxford purloined from Berkshire in the 1970s.

The village's main claim to fame is the Blowing Stone. The stone is in all probability a relic of the Ice Age and was previously situated on White Horse Hill. Martin Atkins, a local squire, brought the large sandstone relic down from its high vantage point and into the shady village of Kingston Lisle. Possibly he was fed up with the noise that blasted forth when experienced lips were placed on one of half a dozen 'rat holes'. It is reported that the sound could be heard seven miles away. The landlord of the local inn, near to where the 3ft high stone resided, decided to cork the holes with wooden blocks that were attached by chains. Perhaps he did not wish to be rudely awakened by drunken pranksters.

Legend associates the Blowing Stone with King Alfred. It is suggested, but in no way proven, that he used it to rouse his scattered chiefs when danger threatened.

The Blowing Stone gained greater fame when Thomas Hughes described it in the opening chapter of *Tom Brown's School Days*. Hughes reports how the landlord of the inn put his mouth to one of the 'rat holes' with great vigour. The author goes on to describe how a gruesome sound between a moan and a roar spread itself over the hillside and into the woods at the back of the house; a ghost-like awful voice. As the innkeeper rose to his feet, purple faced, moans still issued from the stone.

The inn has long been a private residence, but a visitor in the 1970s stated that after several minutes of unsuccessfully trying to obtain some sort of noise from the stone, a small boy emerged from a nearby cottage and successfully produced a call that would have wakened the dead in several counties. It is gratifying to hear that these old country arts have not as yet died out.

There is now a pub named the Blowing Stone Inn at Kingston Lisle, near to the site of the stone.

The Blowing Stone inn sign, Kingston Lisle. (Author's collection)

LITTLE WITTENHAM

Little Wittenham is surrounded by hills, or at least it seems that way. Sinodun Hill (known as Castle Hill) and Harp Hill, stand to each side of the village. It is Sinodun Hill which holds some interest for the enquirer into legend and fable. The hill once held an early fort and has a group of trees, known locally as the Cuckoo's Pen. It is alleged that the trees were planted as a fence to contain a cuckoo. The plan behind this brilliant endeavour was that if the bird could not escape, there would be everlasting summer.

There is a large hollow in the side of Sinodun Hill called the Money Pit. Its name is derived from the local belief that there is a vast horde of treasure buried there. Many have tried to unearth it but have failed. However, it is rumoured that some 200 years ago, a fortune hunter dug so deep that he came across the top of a large chest. As he tried to lift it, a raven swooped down and perched upon it. The raven clearly spoke the words (as ravens do), 'He is not yet born'. The man was naturally scared, decided he was not the chosen one and filled in the hole. Nobody has been able to discover the chest since.

LONG WITTENHAM

In the early 1960s, the Co-operative store at Long Wittenham was the unlikely venue for poltergeist activity. When overnight, it was discovered that various commodities had changed shelves and had even been thrown about the gangway, the management was convinced it was due to a prankster who had remained behind after closing time. Watches were kept, but to no avail. The nocturnal prankster theory was dismissed, and another even less likely reason was put forward. It was thought that slight but regular earth movements could be responsible. What type of tremor could remove large packets of sugar from one shelf and replace them on another beggars all logic.

All such theories were put to flight when one day, the daytime shift watched in amazement as cereal boxes, jam jars and various other commodities left the shelves, slowly circumvented the room and replaced themselves on various other shelves and counters. There were over a dozen instances witnessed by upwards of twenty people. The poltergeist had a special fixation for bicarbonate of soda, which always held a prominent position among the supernatural jugglers' props.

After a week or more of total anarchy and pandemonium, the management decided on an exorcism. The ceremony would seem to have been effective as the spiritual activity slowly ceased. The shelves were restocked but a not wholly convinced staff kept the bicarbonate of soda under lock and key. Nothing untoward has happened since.

One of the author Hilary Stainer Rice's correspondents was a lady from Long Wittenham who inhabited a house at least five centuries old. In 1981, the lady was in bed but well awake pondering on the problems of the day. She turned on her side and noticed what she describes as an oval frame between her bed and that of her husband's. In the frame was the head and shoulders of a woman whose dress and hairstyle dated her as Victorian.

The lady goes on to describe how her eyes met those of the woman in the frame, who seemed somewhat startled by this while the relater of the tale seemed to experience a warm and benign feeling without a shadow of fear. The Victorian lady disappeared as quickly as she had appeared, leaving a dozen questions unanswered. With little or no knowledge of the previous residents of the house, research was impossible. The appearance would seem to have been a one-off; the phantom Victorian lady never returned and will remain one of life's unsolved mysteries.

MAPLEDURHAM

There is very little to the hamlet of Mapledurham other than the large, attractive Mapledurham House (Kenneth Grahame's Toad Hall in *The Wind in the Willows*) and the nearby mill. Both were featured in the *Forsyte Saga* and various other television programmes. It is fitting that such a village should be associated with several ghosts. There is reputed to be a phantom coach and horses that leaves the house at 12 o'clock on New Years' Eve. The spectral coach is heard more often than it is seen. Witnesses have reported uncanny sounds of horses' hooves and metal-rimmed wheels on cobblestones.

A very similar haunting in the vicinity is also heard but rarely seen. A single horse gallops towards the person in a lane named The Warren. The noise of galloping hooves approaches at breakneck speed; witnesses have been known to dive for cover, thinking themselves to be at the mercy of a one-horse stampede. When barely a yard from the victim, whinnying, heavy breathing and snorting are distinctly heard before the phantom steed proceeds down the lane, leaving the witness in total bewilderment.

Hidden in the woods at Mapledurham House is a large, decorative plinth surmounted by a small statue. The statue, for some unknown reason, has been christened 'Old Palm'. Legend dictates that on Christmas Eve, Old Palm comes down from his pedestal and strolls through the village wishing the compliments of the season to the locals. I have yet to find an eyewitness.

Another story is that the plinth marks an underground passage to the house, which was used as an escape route for Catholic priests. Yet another story is that Old Palm was a secret meeting place for the Hell-Fire Club and through the underground passage, Satan could be summoned.

Right: *The plinth at Mapledurham House, Old Palm.* (Author's collection)

Below: *Mapledurham House.* (Author's collection)

In 1854 a 22-year-old Mapledurham serving maid, Louisa Parsons, attended a party at nearby Playhatch. Part way through the lively celebration, Louisa complained of pains in her stomach; the young maid was escorted home where her condition rapidly worsened.

Louisa's parents were simple folk and believed in the ability of Grannie Patin to cure their daughter. Later, after the quack medicine failed to have any effect, a recognised doctor was enlisted. Louisa died the following morning. There is no record of any autopsy taking place. The Parsons decided their daughter had been poisoned at the party. The police were sceptical and nobody was ever charged. The parents were adamant and consulted Grannie Patin for a verse for the tombstone. Grannie supplied the following:

> All you young people as you pass by,
> Pray on my grave now, cast an eye,
> Beware of false lovers and their friends,
> I died from poison you may depend.

The mention of poison upset the local populace; they found the epitaph unseemly and ostracised the Parsons. A certain Dr Hawtry became the rector of Mapledurham. He found the wording offensive enough, but, when he discovered the epitaph had been composed by a witch, his anger knew no bounds. There was a stand-off and then a compromise; much of the offensive wording was removed but Louisa's murderer was never discovered.

Incidentally, buried at Mapledurham is Kenneth Tynan (1927–1980) who devised the nude musical *Oh Calcutta* for the West End. One of his other claims to fame is that he was the first person on television to mouth an obscenity.

NETTLEBED

Nettlebed must be the village with the briefest entry in this book. It is just worth mentioning that Nettlebed was one of the many villages visited by a phantom puma in the mid-1960s.

NORTH MORETON

This pretty South Oxfordshire village, which ironically nestles in the Berkshire Downs, has a very strange if infuriating story to tell.

In 1604, Anne Gunter, a 14 year old girl from North Moreton, was experiencing fits. The cause was undoubtedly 'falling sickness' (epilepsy) but her father, a prominent local businessmen, put his daughter's condition down to witchcraft and ordered some eminent Oxford doctors to examine her. The doctors, specialists in witchcraft, found that Anne suffered from body swelling, temporary deafness and blindness, sneezing and exuded pins and needles from her throat, breasts and fingers. She had also not eaten for twelve days. The cause of Anne's troubles was attributed to Agnes Pepwell, Mary Pepwell and Elizabeth Gregory, three local elderly ladies. Anne's father's determination, along with local feeling, finally necessitated a trial at Abingdon.

All three women were found not guilty. After the trial, Anne was taken into care by the Bishop of Salisbury, Henry Cotton. No doubt she was company to the nineteen children the Bishop already had.

It was Henry Cotton who first discovered Anne's fraud when she supposedly vomited the pins that he had previously marked. On 27 August 1605, the case attracted the attention of King James, who examined the young girl personally. The King sent Anne to the Archbishop of Canterbury's chaplain, a man named Revd Samuel Harsnet, and his friend Dr Edward Jorden. While in the care of these two gentlemen, Anne admitted that she had a natural ailment but her father had encouraged her to exaggerate the condition and make the symptoms more severe by secreting the pins about her person, later to claim she had regurgitated them.

After a year, Sir Edward Gore, the Attorney General, charged Mr Brian Gunter and his daughter with conspiracy.

The infuriating part of this story is that it has no ending. We do know that it was proven Anne was familiar with many books on witchcraft; however, the outcome of the trial is not known.

OUSLEY

Ousley, a vanished village, was supposed to be in the vicinity of Checkendon; although whether it ever existed is doubtful. Legend suggests that the village was mysteriously destroyed by fire during the reign of King Charles I.

The Bells of Ousley, a well-known pub on the River Thames at Old Windsor is a suggested site where brothers from a monastery near Ousley tried to cross with the monastery's bells. The raft overturned and they sank to the bottom. This seems unlikely as the river at Old Windsor is fairly shallow and their bodies would have been discovered by now.

If the Bells of Ousley did exist, it is far more likely that they were being removed to be secreted away during Henry VIII's dissolution of the monasteries. Surely though, it was not necessary to cross the Thames, and if it was, why not go to Henley which is far closer and the river far narrower?

PISHILL

The name of this tiny Oxfordshire hamlet vies with Piddlehampton in Dorset for schoolboy lewd witticisms. In fact, the butt of the jokes is unfounded. The grounds around here were owned by the French family Puis. The corruption is simple and there is no substance whatsoever in the rumour that horses used to drag loads up to the top of the hill before passing water. As one turns the sharp bends of the B480 and comes across the Crown Inn, it is with a feeling of veneration. This is chocolate box, but still Tudor architecture at its best, the exeterior covered by a profusion of wisteria.

The Crown Inn is reputed to possess the largest priest hole in the country and it is from here that a ghost story emerges.

A fugitive priest, thought to be named Dominique, left his concealment for clandestine meetings with an attractive lady guest at the inn. Unfortunately, the lady was married. Dominique would watch from his lofty hiding place for the husband to leave and then shinny down a rope to his and the lady's mutual satisfaction. Inevitably, he was finally caught in a compromising position by the husband and was speedily run through with his sword. Loud footsteps and insistent thumping have been heard in one of the inn's rooms and have been attributed to the luckless Dominique. This is, however, a case of venue and condition being conducive with a story which is, in all probability, a fictional legend.

The Crown Inn, Pishill. (Author's collection)

ROTHERFIELD GREYS

Grey's Court derives its name from Lord de Grey who fought at Crecy. This house was granted a licence to crenellate the building in 1347. When the family line ran out, Henry VIII secured the building for Francis Knollys. Knollys, who became Lord Treasurer to Queen Elizabeth for many years, was a popular man and several roads in the area were named after him. Knolly's son, reported to be a recluse, probably owing to his having a deformed face, succeeded his father in 1596. It is rumoured that he was the model for Shakespeare's Malvolio, steward to Olivia in *Twelfth Night*.

It was during this time that Robert Carr, Earl of Somerset, and a favourite of James I, accompanied by his wife Frances Howard, a well-known beauty, were in forced confinement at Grey's Court during his Majesty's pleasure. Not so heinous a punishment, one would have thought. The pair had been found guilty of murder, having poisoned Sir Thomas Overbury at the Tower of London in 1613.

Today, little remains of the mighty Grey's Court except for the great tower and three smaller ones. However, further buildings have been added over the centuries. Up to the start of the First World War, a 200ft well supplied water to the house; it was raised by a donkey treading a great vertical wheel.

Grey's Court, Rotherfield Greys. (Author's collection)

SOUTH FAWLEY, NEAR WANTAGE

In the late 1960s, South Fawley was a mecca for the meeting of witches. It is also reported that in the same village, a cottage experienced an incessant poltergeist, whose knocking continued for an incredible seventeen years.

SOUTH MORTON

There is a story from South Molton of a farmer who committed suicide. In 1804 William Field hanged himself in his barn. He returned as a ghost and terrified the neighbourhood for nearly fifty years.

In 1850 the situation seemed to be deteriorating; the ghost of the unhappy farmer was becoming more menacing and prolific. No less than eleven clergymen gathered to lay the restless spirit and waited near a pond in the farmyard. However, unbeknown to the clergymen, two farm labourers, brothers James and John Parker, concealed themselves in a pile of straw to watch the proceedings. When the ghost appeared, he demanded to take some living creature with him; he was asked his preference. Either the cockerel on the dunghill or the two mice in the straw, he replied. For some strange reason the clergyman gave him the cockerel (an expensive bird), rather than two worthless mice.

The ghost grabbed the bird and tore it to pieces in anger. The mice he'd expected were the bodies and souls of the Parker brothers. He was disappointed, but being a ghost of honour, he let himself be laid in the pond and a stake was driven through his heart, which is a difficult thing to do with a ghost!

There is also a story of a premonition concerning a white witch. The story goes that in 1894, Felix Maggs, a farmer of South Morton was consulting the witch about his future. The witch informed the worried farmer that she had dreamt that a great black horse would knock him down. Fifteen years later, Maggs was crossing a railway line when he was mowed down and killed by a train.

STANFORD IN THE VALE

This ancient village nestling by the river Ock, Standford, has a very strange story to tell.

A family passing through Stanford in the Vale in 1978 claimed to have been abducted by aliens. The story, which made the daily papers, relates that while driving through the village at 10.15 p.m. one evening, a hovering white light seemed to be keeping pace with the family's car. Later, the spaceship descended in a field beside them. The family, three adults and two children, knew little of what had happened until they found themselves in the same car, just a few miles up the road. On reaching their home in Brockworth, Gloucestershire, they realised that they were at least an hour late; an entire hour had disappeared from their lives.

The driver, the father, returned the next day to try and discover a hedged road he had seen in his trance-like state and any marks in a field where a spacecraft may have landed. He found nothing.

A week later, strange heat spots were irritating the family's skins. The children began to tell of figures they had seen who had escorted the family to the craft and then examined them. There were long and detailed conversations in English with the aliens, who were dressed in close-fitting metallic silver suits and balaclava type helmets. They explained that their own planet was being destroyed and they needed to colonise somewhere else. Under hypnosis, the whole family agreed and every detail seemed to fit, even when they were interviewed separately. The hypnotherapist was most impressed by the consistency of the stories and obviously believed the family. Who knows?

STOKE ROW

Stoke Row is the home of the Maharajah's Well, a picturesque Indian monument built in 1863 by His Highness Ishree Maharajah of Benares, as a token of respect to his friend Edward Reade.

Edward Reade was one of three famous brothers. Charles Reade became a novelist and is most remembered for *The Cloister and the Hearth*. A third brother, John, did well in the Services. The night he died in India, his ghost appeared to his mother at Ipsden House.

STONOR

Stonor Park takes up the vast majority of the hamlet of Stonor. Deer run here in the 150 acres of beech woods. Situated on a knoll in the park is Stonor House, a Tudor brick building with a chapel that contains a priest's hiding hole. The Jesuit Edmund Campion concealed himself here with his secret printing press in the attic. However, he was soon discovered and executed.

The owner once reported to an interviewer about the sound of voices coming from empty rooms, footsteps crossing floors and cupboards being opened by invisible hands. Guests have reported a feeling of being smothered late at night and also the gentle touching of their faces. Dogs will not go near parts of the garden, and if forced to, they begin to shake and whimper and their hair stands on end.

The famous Maharajah's Well, Stoke Row. (Author's collection)

There is also an unusual stone circle here which is said to be haunted and have a curious animal-like smell. Why this should cause surprise when the park is inundated with feral beasts is anyone's guess.

SUTTON COURTENAY

Up until the Second World War, it was not unusual to hear women in Sutton Courtenay and a dozen other nearby villages calling their children home. If the children did not comply, there would be the added threat of 'Hurry up now, or old Danny Grimshaw will get you'.

As every kid knew, if old Danny caught you, he would boil you alive and eat you. That was the terrifying legend; but it quite differs from the facts.

It is true that Danny Grimshaw was hanged for murder in 1824, and it is suspected that the hauntings of such places as Hells Corner and Purgatory Farm were down to Danny. Exorcisms took place in several dark lanes in the Sutton Courtenay area.

Danny Grimshaw was a quiet and taciturn shepherd who spent much of his time with his sheep on the Berkshire Downs. Danny was 22 and married to Anne who was two years his junior. She worked on a farm at Sutton Courtenay where the pair shared a cottage with their baby son William, known as Billy. On 3 January 1824, Danny returned home early after spending a long cold night tending his sheep. Anne was pleased to see him as it gave her the chance to purchase some items from the tiny local shop. Seconds after leaving the cottage, she heard Billy screaming and raced back, accompanied by a neighbour, Catherine Dew. On entering the cottage, the sight they witnessed was horrifying. The baby had been scalded from head to foot with boiling water and was writhing in pain while Danny stood watching, stupified. Billy was rushed to a neighbour, who knew a little about nursing, but within a short period a Dr West was on the scene. West discovered that, apart from the terrible external burns, Billy's lips, gums and throat had also been hideously burned. 'You have poured boiling water down this child's throat,' he accused Danny. 'I don't know what happened,' came the reply, as the father made an exit in a trance-like state.

Edmund Morris, who owned the local paper mill, accompanied by one of his largest workers, made a citizens' arrest on Grimshaw at the Fish Inn several hours later. After ten days of agony, little Billy died.

On 3 March in Reading, Danny was charged with the murder of 6-month-old William Grimshaw. The trial was brief; the prosecution had a dozen witnesses to the fact and as many who had heard him confess. Danny had confessed to the action but claimed it was an accident. On the stand, a shaking Grimshaw stated that he was carrying some boiling water over for shaving, when he had tripped and spilt it all over Billy. Justice Baron Garrow obviously believed Grimshaw and in his lengthy summing up, he pointed out that there were no actual witnesses and no motive whatsoever. He even went on to elaborate about the improbability of guilt and urged the jury not to convict unless they had no doubt whatsoever in their minds.

The jury was having none of it. Blood lust was out and revenge, not justice, ruled the day. The verdict of guilty was quickly reached. The papers described Justice Garrow as very disconsolate as he passed the terrible sentence to which there was no alternative. A pitiful Daniel Grimshaw died on the scaffold at Reading on 4 March 1824. He was 22 and a broken man.

How legend transformed him into a terrifying spectral horseman is open to speculation. It is suggested by Tony Barham in *Witchcraft in the Thames Valley* that the Danny Grimshaw story had been mixed up and intertwined with the legend of Dr Sherwood, another local character who owned a mansion in the area. Apparently Sherwood was a far more heinous character. Unfortunately, very few of his exploits have been recorded.

UFFINGTON

The greatly over-reported Uffington White Horse is the oldest and most enigmatic of the carved hillside equine breeds, its creation dating back to about 100 BC. It is vast and can be seen from a distance of about fifteen to twenty miles away, which has given rise to speculation that it is a sign for the landing of UFOs. The White Horse was not mentioned in the written word until the thirteenth century, when the Abbot of Abingdon Abbey had a bill of sale for land on White Horse Hill.

It has not gone without notice that the famous carving is more akin to a dragon than a horse. This has given rise to the unlikely legend that St George slew the creature on nearby Dragon Hill. Dragon Hill has a patch on it where grass won't grow; this is where allegedly the monster bled to death, thereby stunting the growth of any foliage.

Near to Dragon Hill are two other places of interest: the Manger, a grass-coated ridge, and Uffington Castle, an earthwork and once inhabited Iron Age fort.

As the White Horse has been described in books and magazine reports too numerous to mention, let us concentrate on the improbable story of St George's association with the area, a myth ineptly backed up by a couple of dragon motifs that adorn the doorway of Uffington Church some two miles away. There is also a more modern dragon that embellishes the font. This is an extremely tenuous association as there must be similar motifs on churches the length and breadth of the country.

St George is reputed to have been born in Coventry. He joined the Crusades and fought in the Holy Land. While there, he slayed a terrible dragon, thereby saving a king's daughter whom he later married and brought back to Coventry, where they lived happily ever after.

The sparse facts tell a totally different story. England's patron saint was not English and never laid sight on Coventry. He was born early in the fourth century at Lydda in Palestine when the Emperor Diocletian's great persecution broke out. George publicly declared himself a Christian and refused to take part in the pagan sacrifices. This brought about his downfall; he was tortured and then decapitated at Nicomedia on 23 April.

The dragon story did not appear until 1275, in a fictitious publication called the *Golden Legend*. This has George residing in the town of Silene in Libya. There an angry dragon was pacified by the townsfolk who left out two sheep at night. Finally the sheep ran out and the monster demanded a fresh and plump young virgin to satisfy his hunger. Lots were drawn and on the fourth night, a local princess got unlucky and was led to her doom. George was having none of this and appeared from behind a bush with his lance. After many days of battle, the dragon fell, badly wounded. The victorious George led him into town where he summarily decapitated the beast. The appreciative king gave George his daughter as his bride. Make of these stories what you will.

I will not move on without describing some of the celebrations and sports enacted during the 'Scouring of the White Horse'. Thomas Hughes, Tom Brown's creator, goes into some detail in his tale of that name. I have also read a colourful account by Cecilia Millson in her *Tales of Old Berkshire*. The accounts

The strange dragon motifs at Uffington Church, Uffington. (Author's collection)

tell of backswording, with combatants arriving from as far afield as Somerset and Wiltshire, including men famous in their time – Blackford of Swindon, Tom Black of Inkpen and Corporal Shaw. The sport was simplicity itself: contestants had one arm tied behind their backs and a cudgel in the other. The object of the sport was to split your opponent's head open.

Apparently the women were not interested in this blood sport. They found it more amusing to see the eight or a dozen blindfolded men trying to catch a man with a bell attached to his waist. There was also a competition for women to see who could smoke the most tobacco in an hour. As women became more ladylike, the entries grew less. Only two gypsy women entered in 1808 and the challenge was dropped. Wrestling, cheese rolling, heavy carthorse racing, donkey racing and a competition for men to take a bullet from a barrel of flour added to the merriment. Grinning through a horse's collar was a popular pastime. Hurling was also in vogue as was chasing a cartwheel from the top of the manger. Cecilia Millson pointed out that bowling for a pig was too tame for these hardy peasants. Rolling and wrestling to grab a greased pig was more to their liking.

It is said that the evening was the most romantic as the local lads grabbed the girls and whirled them off their feet. This seems doubtful when you imagine a girl being grabbed by a fellow who has spent most of the day in the beer tent. Possibly he had wandered out to get a cracked skull from a cudgel, a bloody nose from the boxing booth, fallen head over heels at the hurdles and was covered in flour from the barrel. And what about when he put a hand around the girl's waist which had recently held a greased pig?

WALLINGFORD

Records show that during the Civil War, the town of Wallingford was crowded with drunken brawling troops. This being the case, the authorities thought it prudent to place a gallows at the end of the town. It seems that this had the desired calming effect.

The George is a prominent building in the thriving little town of Wallingford. It is known that a man called Hobson was murdered at the inn in 1626 but it is not his shade that haunts the George.

A strange feature in one of the bedrooms; known as the Teardrop Room because of the unusual décor – a wall which has a peculiar design likened to large teardrops – has given rise to intense speculation. The legend is that many years ago, the landlord's daughter was infatuated with a young man of the town. The couple were soon to be married and prospects looked good. While inspecting his new bridal home, the young man was attacked by burglars and bludgeoned to death. Rumour was rife that the landlord was involved but no one was ever charged. On hearing the sad news, the bride's grief led to her insanity. She was confined to her room where her tortured mind was in such disarray that she spent the rest of her days painting weird murals, her designs constructed from tears and soot, her paintbrush her fingers and hair.

Guests have given quite graphic accounts of a wailing woman they have at first mistaken for a member of staff. The apparition soon fades and disappears into the masonry of the Teardrop Room, leaving the observer with an overpowering feeling of depression and remorse.

At Gould's Heath near Wallingford lived Martha Pearce, a well-respected clairvoyant and witch. However, few if any took notice of Martha when she foresaw a rail crash at Hampton Gate on Christmas Eve 1874. The crash resulted in thirty-one deaths.

WANTAGE

William Berridge, landlord of the Blue Boar at Wantage, was about to close for the night on 30 August 1833. Custom was sparse; just two locals, a French boy called Marriot and his friend, George King; a sulky, churlish and fat itinerant bean cutter, a fact borne out by a large and sharp bean hook the scruffy individual carried with him. Berridge knew the lad was staying with fellow licensee Mrs Pullin at the nearby White Hart. This night, the lad's arrogance had gone; he was physically shaking as he pulled out his purse. Significantly, the landlord noticed a bent sixpence among the coins.

King, lately of Cumnor near Oxford, was known to Marriot, who could not get rid of his companion. King, now petrified and quivering, uncontrollably offered Marriot money to find him a place to stay. They tried several inns and lodgings but were out of luck. Reluctantly, Marriot, who slept in a blacksmith's stables, permitted King to stay the night. They broke company the following morning with King heading for Court Farm at Hanney.

At the White Hart, James Pullin, aged 12, got up early on 31 August. He was going fishing and was very quiet, as he did not wish to wake his mother, Ann, or his half-sister. Opening the door of the bar parlour, young James came across the most appalling sight. Across the blood-soaked carpet lay the body of 40-year-old Ann Pullin. Some 4ft away lay her decapitated head with its neat white bonnet still attached. Later inspection by a Constable Jackson discovered that the landlady's keys were missing and that her purse had been cut from her gown. It took little time for the populace to suspect that the itinerant lodger was responsible for the atrocity. He had been witnessed spending lavishly in the Wantage inns and William Berridge was soon to report the bent sixpence, an item that friends told the police Ann had kept for good luck.

George King was found hiding in a bean field at Court Farm and was arrested by two farm labourers, specially sworn in for this purpose. King was approached with caution, as one would, seeing that he had a bean hook capable of decapitating one's head at a single blow.

Most of the town was disgusted when Ann Pullin's family saw an eye for business by exhibiting Ann's separated head and body for the price of a pint. There was no shortage of ghoulish customers.

After a brief enquiry on 2 September, King was charged and so far having offered very little co-operation, was remanded to the Lent Assizes at Reading. It is twenty-eight miles from Wantage to Reading, and while King was being transported something strange happened.

It was a thirsty trip and a journey thwart with danger. Along the route, Constables Jackson and Jones were protecting King from both physical and verbal abuse, as one paper recounted: 'They gave very manifest symptoms of their execration of so foul a deed.'

The small party pulled into the Bull at Streatley. King, who was shackled at the ankles, was taken in and supplied with ale. All of a sudden, the prisoner arose and approached a picture of a middle-aged woman. 'Those damned eyes, they follow you wherever you go.'

It was the first time that King had shown the slightest emotion. Now shaking and cringing, he cried: 'Those bloody eyes, Mrs Pullin's eyes, following me about the room.' George knelt behind a chair as the officers tried to pacify him. 'I can see the eyes, Mrs Pullin's eyes, staring from her head, watching me, accusing me.' Jones shunted bewildered customers out of the room. Jackson got out his notebook – at last, a confession.

There was no doubt that King would be found guilty – and at Reading in late February 1834 he was. Mr Justice Patterson donned the black cap and sentenced King to be hanged on 3 March.

King met his maker with his natural sullen attitude and without saying a word. George King's body was given to the surgeons, the usual outcome for the remains of a hanged man. A large fissure was found encroaching on his brain, the result of an earlier farm accident. Possibly, in more enlightened times, X-rays might have revealed a greater insight into the young man's behaviour.

One famous figure who has made his way into fiction, Dick Whittington, married a Wantage girl, Alex Fitzwarren; luckily for Dick, she was a very wealthy lady. The story of the pantomime, based on a play written in 1605, 183 years after Whittington's death, has not a grain of truth in it. It is true that our hero left for London from Pauntley in Gloucestershire at the age of 13, but, being the son of Sir William Whittington, he travelled in style surrounded by goods and servants. There is no doubt that Richard had a fine start in the capital. A letter of introduction to Sir John Fitzwarren, a wealthy mercer (cloth dealer) did not go

Dick Whittington. (B. Allaway)

amiss. Whittington was made mayor of the capital on three occasions and lent money to several kings. Whether or not this had any bearing on his progress is a matter of conjecture. There was no knighthood, no 'turn again Dick Whittington, Lord Mayor of London', and, sadly, no black cat.

Wantage has one of the few road casualty ghosts. There is a strange shortage of them, considering the carnage there has been over the years. A man in a cap and overcoat steps out in front of vehicles on the outskirts of the town. There is so little warning that it is impossible to avoid him. However, there is no sound of a collision, and as vehicles pass through him, there is no bump, and those brave enough to pull up and return to the spot, find no body. I have found no record of a pedestrian being killed here.

WATLINGTON

Watlington lies at the foot of the Chilterns, half surrounded by mighty beech trees, and a stone's throw away from Icknield Way, the oldest road in England.

There is a mysterious hill figure here, cut out of the chalk. It is the shape of an obelisk and a landmark for miles around. There is a school of thought that believes the white mark was cut by an eighteenth- or nineteenth-century local eccentric. There may have been such a person who scoured and cleaned it, and brought it back to a more reasonable condition, but the original is much older and its closeness to the Icknield Way is no coincidence. In those days, travellers were guided by such landmarks. There is a third and much supported idea that the carving was a phallic symbol, a large and visual appreciation of the gods of fertility.

WATCHFIELD

At 11 p.m. on 20 July 1893, 9-year-old Thomas Carter lay in bed with his younger brother listening to an almighty row between his parents; a not unusual event. At just after 11.30 p.m., he heard his mother Rhoda cry, 'No, John, no!', then almost beseechingly, 'Lord have mercy on me,' followed by silence.

The Carter children, who were farmer boys, were up at 4.30 a.m. the following morning to do their chores. Afterwards, as they ate their breakfast, Thomas noticed his father acting in an unusual way. He had lugged a large bath and firewood into the smithy that adjoined the cottage. These items were followed by two more; a pitchfork and a shovel. Both boys knew better than to question their father so they made their way to school in silence.

Mrs Titcombe, Rhoda's mother, lived with her son Dave a few yards away. At 9 a.m. on 21 July, she knocked on Carter's door but got no reply. Through the window though, she could see Rhoda's new green coat hanging on the kitchen door. Also, only three breakfasts had been laid on the table. Turning, she saw Carter leaving the smithy. She enquired of Rhoda. 'Gone to her sisters at Eastleech' came the surly reply. She was then ignored. 'How long will she be gone?' 'Didn't say, day or two.' Carter entered and closed the smithy door.

Anne Butler, Rhoda's friend, was hanging out clothes when she noticed thick black smoke accompanied by a sickly stench coming from the smithy. Anne crossed the road and hammered on the smithy door. 'Where is Rhoda?' enquired Anne. 'Go away, you are a loose woman. Rhoda's up at Eastleech', was the reply.

Later that day, Thomas Carter was despatched to fetch 28lbs of coal. Mrs Titcombe intercepted his passage and enquired about her daughter. His lack of knowledge made her very suspicious indeed.

When smoke was seen gushing from the smithy again on 22 July, Dave Titcombe knocked on the door. Not being satisfied with Carter's explanation that he was boiling up offal, Dave decided to make the thirty mile round trip to Eastleech by bike and also to send Anne Butler for the police.

PC Sparkes made a couple of cursory calls at Carter's farm, without finding John Carter. He was pretty sure that Rhoda was alright and that her brother would have found her at Eastleech. When news came to the contrary, he became alarmed and made a successful effort at contacting Carter. He searched the farm in Carter's presence and became very suspicious. 'She's left me,' stated Carter. Sparkes thought to himself that it was strange that a woman would depart leaving all her good clothes behind.

On 25 July, Carter had a drink with his brother in Wantage and confessed to him that he had killed his wife. At 9 a.m. on 26 July, after wrestling with his conscience all night, Carter's brother walked into Wantage police station and reported Carter's confession.

John Carter was arrested at 11 a.m. Shortly after, Sergeant Benning and PC Sparkes searched Carter's barn. Three inches under the floor, Rhoda's body was discovered, the nose smashed and with horrific bruising around the throat. The body had been burned and boiled.

Between appearing at Wantage and his actual trial at Reading in November 1893, speculation was rife concerning the disappearance of Carter's previous wife.

Carter had stated that his previous wife (his second), had walked out on him four years previously. Suspicion had been high. What type of woman would walk out on a 5-year-old child and a baby? A massive search was orchestrated at Burnt Lease, Carter's previous home, but nothing was discovered.

At Reading on 16 November, Carter pleaded not guilty. He claimed he had lashed out at Rhoda but the prosecution proved that she had died of strangulation. Carter's defence team tried for manslaughter but it was a pathetic attempt against the mounting evidence.

The jury were out for just a few minutes before returning a guilty verdict. John Carter was hanged at Reading Gaol on 3 December 1893.

Of the disturbing disappearance of Carter's second wife, nothing more was heard. Carter's first wife had died in a suspicious accident on a farm where they had worked. Not a lucky man with wives, John Carter.

There was a quaint old custom in Watchfield concerning the scaring off of witches. Residents of the village hung a sprig of St John's Wort around the necks of small children on Midsummer's Eve, when witches' curses were thought to be at their most potent. I can find no trace of the practice today.

WEST HENDRED

West Hendred is one of many charming villages wrested from Berkshire in the 1960s. There is a strange inscription on the church window here. It is from a grateful glazier and states: 'I Parker glazed this church in 1784, and glad of the job.' Incidentally, down the road at West Challow, the county's oldest church bell states, 'Paul the Potter made me.'

In West Hendred, take it easy through the streets here; a lonely ghost dressed in a cap and overcoat might dash out in front of your car.

WITHERIDGE HILL, NEAR HIGHMOOR CROSS

A track through the woods at Witheridge Hill leads to a low stone wall where there have been several well authenticated sightings of a ghostly woman, identity unknown, sitting and brooding.

2

CENTRAL OXFORDSHIRE

AMBROSDEN

The Church of St Mary's had its foundation laid in a field named Church Leys. However, it appears that the Devil had not been consulted on the proposed site and out of cussedness, strongly disapproved. This being the case, building materials left overnight for use the following day were transported some several hundred yards away. After several futile attempts of transporting them to the original site, the labourers gave up and the Devil had his way.

BABLOCK HYTHE

This is a pretty hamlet on the Thames made famous by the *Scholar Gypsy*. Bablock Hythe is supposed to be the place where Joseph Glanvill (1636–1680) had his spectre gypsy do a small experiment in the supernatural.

Glanvill was probably the first unbiased student of witchcraft and the supernatural. After taking his degree at Oxford University in 1658, he spent years studying witchcraft, even living with covens in Somerset. Glanvill also collected and correlated supposedly true tales of hauntings as he travelled the country. He was probably the first writer of ghost stories as we know them today.

One such story tells of an Oxford student, who, bored with university academia, forsook his future and wandered with the gypsies, as in Matthew Arnold's *Scholar Gypsy*:

> Who tired of knocking on perferment's door,
> One summer morn forsook,
> His friends, and went to learn the gypsy lore,
> And roam'd the world with that wild brotherhood,
> And came as most men deem'd to little good,
> But came to Oxford and his friends no more.

The Scholar Gypsy at Bablock Hythe. (B. Allaway)

The Scholar Gypsy had been roaming the moors and the Thames Valley near Bablock Hythe for some 200 years before Arnold penned his famous poem. He had seemingly learned many things from that wild brotherhood, including eternal life.

It was in the vicinity of Bablock Hythe that the Scholar Gypsy, or perhaps his spirit, came across two Oxford graduates at a lone alehouse. He conducted an experiment by getting them to indulge in a hushed conversation in one room while he sat in the far corner of another. He later repeated the conversation word for word. When asked how he had performed such a feat, he replied that it was simple. He had decided what they were to think and then placed his words in their mouths. Before his explanation could be pursued, the gypsy had thrown his grey cloak over his face and disappeared into the night.

This most romantic of apparitions was to be witnessed on countless occasions in North Berkshire and South Oxfordshire over two centuries, Bablock Hythe being a favourite place of his for meditation. As Arnold describes:

Matthew Arnold.

For most I know thou lov'st retired ground,
Thee, at the ferry, Oxford riders Blythe,
Returning home on summer nights have met,
Crossing the stripling Thames at Bablock Hythe.

BAMPTON

It is stated that the Morris dancing tradition at Bampton has been unbroken for over 500 years. Also, for as many as 200 years, the leading fiddlers came from the same family, and may still do so. The Bampton Morris dancers are unusual, if not unique in having an additional figure, a sword bearer who carries his decorated foil with a tin containing cake at the end. The cake is a representation of an animal's head, which in years gone by would have been sliced and passed to the spectators; as the cake is sliced now.

BICESTER

For such an ancient little town, I was mildly surprised that Bicester didn't have more to offer a student of the supernatural. It does, however, boast a couple of ghost stories.

The Crock Well lay near the boundary of Bicester House. After several near fatal accidents, the well was covered by a concrete slab and a pump was put in its place. This safer modernisation took place about the turn of the twentieth century. A Spanish-looking gentleman is said to haunt the site. The phantom has been seen on quite a regular basis and seems to specialise in appearing to courting couples. One such couple in 1920 described the apparition as looking like the figure on a famous port wine bottle.

Could this Spanish (or Portuguese) looking gentleman resemble the Cavalier that is reputed to have fallen to his death down the well shaft? This unfortunate gentleman is said to have met his untimely demise while being pursued by Cromwell's troops.

Bicester's second ghost also has associations with both Bicester House and the Civil War. The Roundheads, having reached Bicester House, were determined to plunder it. The lady of the house had been left in charge, the menfolk being away with the Royalists. Under interrogation, this lady refused to disclose the whereabouts of the family valuables. She had previously secreted the heirlooms in Rookery Pond when she heard of the Parliamentarians' approach. For refusing to tell, she was put to the sword. For many years her spirit returned to search for

The Crockwell entrance, Bicester.

the treasure, accompanied by her favourite white horse. If this poor lady is still searching Rookery Pond, she has a thankless job; there has been a fire station on the site for a number of years.

BINSEY

King Henry VIII and Katherine of Aragon were among the grand and famous that visited St Margaret's Well at Binsey. Legend dictates that the well water could restore fertility in barren women; it is also reputed to cure eye disorders. Unfortunately, it has deteriorated into a wishing well.

I delved into the history of the well. The story goes that the Pagan ruler of Leicester, Algar, had been blinded by stoning for seizing the hand of St Ferediswyde. He secretly called on St Margaret for help, who in turn blessed the well. Algar bathed his eyes and, miraculously, his sight was restored. Where the fertility aspect comes from is unknown.

BURFORD

Burford, this most beautiful Cotswold town, is as antiquated as it is picturesque. It was of vast importance in ancient Wessex when armies of the town defeated

The healing well at St Margaret's Church, Binsey. (Author's collection)

Ethelbald of Mercia in AD 753. It was 1226 before the old priory was officially mentioned, but there is believed to have been a hospital on the site prior to this.

Both the priory and neighbouring rectory have been sites of poltergeist activity over the years. Even the quiet prayers of the Benedictine sisters who now inhabit the priory have done little to exorcise the activity.

Throughout their history, doors slamming, footsteps, wall knockings, bells ringing, piercing screams and apparitions have been the lot of both the priory and rectory. The unusual noises have been blamed on a black-cassocked monk who has been seen on rare occasions over the years.

Although this small, cowled brother seems to favour a position next to a huge fireplace near the entrance hall, he and his actions have been witnessed in every conceivable corner of the old building. Nothing is known of this monk, but he may have been the perpetrator of a hideous murder that is reputed to have taken place in the rectory. The piercing scream that is occasionally heard is also attributed to this murder. With the immense amount of history that has been attached to Burford priory, any number of colourful personalities could be responsible for the supernatural activities.

When Henry VIII dissolved the monasteries, Burford became the property of a barber/surgeon named Edmund Harman. Harman never lived at Burford but it is thought that his staff performed there for a short while. The old priory was involved in the Civil War, with both Parliamentarian and Royalist troops visiting it on separate occasions. Charles II dared to call here infrequently, but Nell Gwynne was a far more regular caller.

There is a better documented murder at Burford priory and one that is a fine example of a miscarriage of justice. In 1695, the priory was owned by Lord Abercorn, who was tried and rather suspiciously acquitted of the murder of John Prior. Lord Abercorn had quarrelled violently with Prior minutes before the victim's body was found in the summerhouse overlooking the monks' burial ground. Instead, Lord Abercorn's gardener was tried, convicted and hanged for the same murder. It was thought that he was a scapegoat and that it is his ghost that walks the grounds of Burford priory. The mystical spirit of this unnamed gardener/gamekeeper has been witnessed on many occasions by nuns, guests and visitors alike. The spectre carries an old-fashioned gun and is accompanied by an overwhelming feeling of depression.

Is this unquiet spirit the manifestation of a greatly wronged man, a man convicted of his employer's guilt? If so, he may slowly be accepting the inevitable. The spectral gardener is making fewer appearances as time goes on.

The town of Burford is purported to be haunted by the strangest of all phenomenon. It is unique because it takes the form of a dark cloud which descends swiftly like a black fog on local roads, causing people that drive through it to experience the most instense feeling of depression and a threatening melancholy, verging on suicidal.

Burford priory, Burford. (Author's collection)

Dogs travelling through the cloud tremble and become alarmed to such an extent that they are virtually uncontrollable. The cloud ascends as swiftly as it descends, taking whatever strange and menacing powers it exudes with it.

Burford is also reported to have a phantom coach. Inside this ghostly spectre sits wicked Sir Lawrence Tanfield and his equally insufferable wife. Sir Lawrence, an allegedly corrupt judge and lawyer, became rich enough to purchase Burford priory in 1617. Then as lord of the manor, he set about depriving the local populace of their rights.

The pair were hated during their earthbound existence and their spirits plagued the town after their demise. It took seven priests, complete with bell, book and candle to capture this forceful spectral couple and lay them to rest under one of the arches of Burford Bridge. The spirit of Lady Tanfield was so violent that it had to be corked in a bottle. Legend dictates that if ever the river underneath the arch runs dry, the hated pair will return. One dry season many years later, the river almost ran dry and the townsfolk began to panic.

Heinous as the Tanfields may have been, there is a rather fine effigy of them in Burford Church.

CATMORE

In the early to mid-1960s, a witchcraft group existed in Oxford. The mainstay of this group was an appreciator of Aleister Crowley, who called himself Lord Boleskin.

Lord Boleskin decided on a grand gathering of the brotherhood in a wood near Catmore, on the Downs near Oxford. Tony Barham informs us that the event was marred by heavy showers. A cockerel that had been brought for sacrifice, sensing its imminent doom, escaped from a cardboard box and attacked all and sundry before bolting. A large sheet of hardboard painted with mythical beings blew over and became a sodden mess. Obviously the inclement weather was not conducive to the lighting of candles. The only people who enjoyed themselves were a group of scoffers who had followed by taxi and found fertile ground for their insults. Against such odds, Lord Boleskin and his following called it a day and retreated.

CHADLINGTON

A Bronze Age stone, the 8ft high Hawkstone, stands on a remote ridge about a mile north of the village.

CHARLBURY

The Phantom Grey of Charlbury is the name of the spectral stallion that is believed to haunt the lanes near the village. The grey appears white in colour as it is picked up by car headlights late at night.

To the astonishment of motorists, the phantom stallion prances beside their car for several seconds before leaping vast hedges beside the road. One lady motorist was so concerned about the beast's safety after seeing it leap a 7ft embankment, that she made enquiries in the village. To her surprise, the villagers showed little concern; 'That'll be the Phantom Grey,' they briefly replied, before returning to their chores.

CHARLTON ON OTMOOR

The marshes around Otmoor give a distinct feeling of vulnerable remoteness on windy autumn days. But in late spring, Charlton on Otmoor, on the edge of the marsh, is a joy to behold, containing a fine collection of thatched seventeenth-century cottages and stone farmhouses. The church is its focal point and its

Charlton on Otmoor, home of the famous May Queen ceremony. (Author's collection)

unfortunate history of Cromwell's men tearing down the gallery and rood is easily forgotten on a May Day morning.

This is a day of garland dressings, processions, May Queens and dancers and most of all, it is a day for the children. Prizes are given for sporting events, dances and May Day crosses. The crosses are cut by the children, covered in flowers and hung with garlands on a clipped yew cross that is supported by a rood screen. Long may it continue.

CUMNOR

Amy Robsart: did she fall or was she pushed, strangled or possibly poisoned? We shall never know. All was hushed up; the enquiry was a sham.

All that remains now of her home are a few feet of derelict wall and a fireplace adjoining Cumnor Church. Eight years after her marriage to Robert Dudley, Amy moved from Lincoln to Berkshire to take up the charming abode her husband had provided. Robert Dudley was the MP for Abingdon and a favourite with Queen Elizabeth I. There had been rumours of Dudley and the Queen for some time. They mattered little to his charming wife. She busied herself with household management, assisted by Anthony Foster, Dudley's steward.

On Sunday 8 September 1560, a mop fair was being held at Abingdon. With Robert being away, Amy gave the whole of her staff permission to attend. She would be quite safe, attended by three lady friends.

Two of the lady friends left early, the third at 9 p.m. Amy was to be in the house on her own between then and 11 p.m., when the staff would return.

At 11.30 p.m., a surprised group of servants found their mistress's body at the foot of the stairs in Cumnor Place. Her neck had been broken, there were signs of strangulation around her throat, and her lips were blue and singed as if poison had been forcibly administered. Dudley's reactions at the loss of his wife were strange indeed. He heard the news the following day at Windsor Castle, where he was being entertained by the Queen. He did not go home himself, but sent his cousin Sir Thomas Blount to investigate. He also sent his wife's body for burial at Oxford, a most lavish affair, but strangely, unattended by Dudley.

Rumour was rife and well justified. The whole of Europe enjoyed the scandal. Dudley's name was associated with the Queen's at every possible level. Quite well substantiated plots were elaborated upon with relish. Sir Blount's half-hearted investigation was a charade and was met with a convenient wall of silence. A persistent rumour (probably closer to the truth) was that Anthony Foster had lain in hiding with an accomplice. When Amy's friends had left, they had tried to poison and then strangle her before finally throwing her down the stairs.

Despite the conspirators' closing of ranks, a little evidence did seep through. An Oxford physician was approached for a physic by one of Dudley's servants. The man stated that Amy was very ill but the doctor knew this not to be the case. He refused, fearing for his own safety. The next day, Amy died. Unfortunately, the physician's fear prevented him revealing the facts for seven years. Bombarded by bribes and threats, the jury dissolved after issuing a statement that 'after a searching enquiry they could find no presumption of evil doing'. There is little else to relate.

Dudley married again and Queen Elizabeth I was furious. Dudley attempted to poison his second wife and then bigamously went through a third marriage ceremony. Elizabeth was so livid, she slapped his face before the entire court and threatened to throw him into the Tower. Dudley absconded and sank into obscurity for seven years. In 1585, we find him yet again forgiven by the monarch and playing an uninspired part in the war against Spain. Once again, wealthy and popular Dudley prospered, but his health was suspect. In 1588, he was riding in Wychwood Forest when legend relates that he was approached by the ghost of Amy Robsart. He returned to his home at Cornbury Park where he died five days later – a terrified man.

There is far more evidence of Amy Robsart haunting Cumnor. Shortly after her death, terrifying screams were heard from the staircase where she had met her demise. Tenants came and went with extreme rapidity, all complaining of the horrifying shrieks. Dudley never stayed another night in Cumnor Place. The ominous old house remained empty for years, solely tenanted by Amy's screaming spirit. At one time, nine priests came down from Oxford to exorcise the un-quiet spirit and to lay it to rest in a nearby pool, later known as Lady Dudley's pond. The exorcism was a failure and the house lay uninhabited for decades, inevitably falling into disrepair. In 1814, Cumnor Place was deemed dangerous and was demolished, but as recently as the 1980s, short sharp screams have been heard from where the old staircase once stood.

As late as 1970, it was alleged that black magic thrived in Cumnor. The papers had a field day when the mutilated bodies of several sheep were found in the vicinity. Tony Barham in *Witchcraft in the Thames Valley* suggests that since the days of Amy Robsart, Cumnor has thrived on its air of atmospheric mystery. Barham quotes from the ancient ballad:

> The village maids, with fearful glance
> Avoid the ancient moss grown wall
> Nor ever lead the merry dance
> Among the groves of Cumnor Hall.

ENSTONE

Enstone is actually comprised of two villages facing each other across the river Glyme – Church Enstone and Neat Enstone. Here is one of the oldest tithe barns in the country, dating from 1382, and a church containing Norman and Saxon masonry. There is a strange, ancient chambered tumulus a couple of stringent miles to the west, and south of the villages is the difficult to find Hoar Stone, described by experts as a collapsed dolmen tucked beneath a tree in a hedge. I personally saw it thirty years ago and even then, its future seemed in jeopardy.

EYNSHAM

An Eynsham house once had a painting depicting a wedding in 1541. A boy named William married a girl called Mary. William had just turned 11 and Mary was four years older.

FIFIELD

The Merry Mouth has an interesting inn sign at Fifield. The hamlet was once owned by a gentleman named Fifield Murimuth, the name over the years becoming 'merry mouth'.

FINSTOCK

A well at Finstock has been worshipped, although officially forbidden, since AD 963. Also, local children make a concoction of liquorice and water at nearby Wychwood Forest Road.

FULBROOK

A local myth relates that in the eighteenth century, there were three robber brothers at Fulbrook; Tom, Dick and Harry Dunsden were the scourge of Wychwood Forest. The brothers were said to inhabit a cottage at Icombe that had an underground passage to a cave where a local smithy shod their horses. One of the gang's most notorious successes was to rob the Oxford to Gloucester stagecoach of some £500. Less successful was a plan to rob Tangley Manor during the absence of the family. Unfortunately for the brothers, they discussed their plans while drinking in a local pub. Somebody overheard them and reported the story to the stoic butler, who in turn informed local constables. All stood in wait in the manor.

Late at night, the Dunsdens approached and Dick put his hand through a hole they had cut near a window. As Dick reached for the key, a constable slipped a rope over his wrist; a tug of war ensued. The constable managed to secure the arm to some nearby furniture.

'Cut! Cut!' screamed a voice from outside; this the villains did and an arm fell into the house. The brothers fled, leaving behind a trail of blood. Dick was never seen again and it must be assumed that he died of his wounds. Tom and Harry were captured years later in 1784 at Gloucester, where they were hanged. Their bodies were then returned to Oxfordshire where they were gibbeted on an oak tree at Habbergallows Hill.

I must point out that other than the dates of the hangings at Gloucester, there is very little evidence to substantiate this story.

GODSTOW

Just north of Oxford lies the tiny hamlet of Godstow. It is famous for two buildings, the Trout Inn and the ruined Benedictine nunnery.

Probably the most famous of the many celebrities that have visited the Trout over the centuries is Lewis Carroll, author of *Alice in Wonderland* and *Alice Through the Looking Glass*. The actual Alice was Alice Liddell, who, accompanied by her sisters, was a regular guest on Carroll's little boat.

The ruined nunnery at Godstow, reputedly haunted by the mournful Fair Rosamund. (Author's collection)

Another celebrity at the Trout was Matthew Arnold, who could see his *Dreaming Spires of Oxford* from the terrace. Yet another celebrity, who seems none too fond of the inn, was Thomas Hearne. In 1732, the famous Oxford historian described a fair at the Trout thus: 'booths and vicious living were there and puppet shews and rope dancing to the debauching and corrupting of youth'.

From the ruined nunnery comes the tale of Fair Rosamund. Rosamund was the daughter of Walter de Clifford and the mistress of Henry II whom he left guarded at Woodstock by the King's Knight, Sir Thomas. While Henry and his son were fighting in France, Queen Eleanor seized the chance to murder Sir Thomas and force Rosamund to drink from a poisoned chalice. Rosamund was murdered in 1175 and her body was buried at Godstow. However, in 1191, the body was exhumed and buried outside the church in unconsecrated grounds. Could this be the reason behind the smiling spirit that has often been seen crossing the river and disturbing the peacocks? Could this be the shade of the lovely fair Rosamund?

HEADINGTON

Headington, now a suburb of Oxford, is famous for its Morris Men. It is also well known, strangely, for its shark. The shark is 25ft long, made out of fibreglass and adorns a gentleman's roof. After a long legal fight and endless hours of debate, it seems it will now remain there for the foreseeable future. It appears that Oxford Town Council thought that it would be denying creativity and expression in this pinnacle of academia if it enforced the shark's removal.

Something fishy at Headington. (Author's collection)

HORSEPATH, NEAR WHEATLEY

John Harris, a ghost hunter and renowned author, has told of a strange story that happened to some friends of his at Horsepath. It concerned a family with a young boy that moved into the area. The child began to talk of a friend he had made but did not know his name. The boy described his new acquaintance as having long fair hair. The mother thought little of this and was soon busy with other things. Her son, in fact, had half a dozen young friends in the neighbourhood. The nameless boy, who was regularly in the garden, caused no comment. The mother saw the top of a blond head passing her window on three occasions. On one such occasion, she shouted to him, saying that her son was already up the lane playing with some of his friends. The child took no notice and continued walking. Thinking he had not heard, the young mother opened the door to inform him. As she rounded the corner of the house, the blond-haired boy slowly vanished in front of her eyes.

IFFLEY

I am indebted to Tony Barham for this charming little story concerning Iffley in Oxfordshire. Back in the early twentieth century, the villagers of Iffley were concerned about a ghost who walked the streets by night. The few who had seen the spectre described him as being a man with a floppy hat and a stump for a missing leg. It was the stump that caused the problem, because its continual rhythmic clatter on the pavement woke up the good people of the village.

The elders of the community approached the local clergy with a view to exorcism. The clergy refused, for what reason we are not informed. Not despairing, the elders approached an old man who slept on a bench at Cowley. This impromptu exorcist had been a valet to an ex-naval gentleman but had lost his job and had fallen on hard times. In due course, the exorcist arrived, much to the delight of the populace.

However, when the brave dispeller of evil was shown where the ghost walked and was furnished with a graphic description of his less than alluring characteristics, he began to talk of leaving. Alarm set in and the villagers decided that Dutch courage was the order of the day. This having been provided in copious amounts from the local alehouse, moral fibre returned. The exorcist's remedy for evil casting was unorthodox indeed. It entailed him standing in the centre of the village, waving an ancient bicycle pump and threatening to fight anybody that passed by. Finally, the exorcist was arrested and charged with blocking the highway and being drunk and disorderly. As far as I can ascertain, no further attempts were made at exorcism and the one-legged spectre still clatters his way up the streets of Iffley occasionally.

Iffley, where an unusual exorcism took place. (Author's collection)

KENNINGTON

Kennington is too close to large towns to be a distinct village. There are three rather brief but unusual stories attached to the area. Here they appear as I heard them.

In 1762, two local men who had been involved in a feud for many years, decided to sort it out once and for all with rounds of fisticuffs. They fought for hours, crossing the Isis back and forth as each attempted to gain the upper hand, until, finally, one combatant named Hen-Toe, submitted. It was later reported that, 'We hear he is since dead.'

A second story that I have heard many times and have used before in *A Grim Almanac of Old Berkshire* concerns a certain Mr Broom. In 1786, Mr Broom of Kennington arose early, woke his wife, placed a halter around her neck and dragged her to Littlemore. There he sold her to a man called Pantin for 5s. There was a large family called Pantin in the area with several members involved in witchcraft. However, Pantin could have been none too pleased with his purchase, for a little later he gave her away to a woodman in Bagley Woods.

Bagley Woods sprang to fame (or notoriety) in 1893 when a woman's decomposed body was discovered. Some Kennington men came forward stating that they had heard a Bagley woodsman threaten to do for his wife after previously kicking her in the jaw. No one was ever charged.

Isambard Kingdom Brunel, one of those rescued from a Great Western train in 1852. (B. Allaway)

I am indebted to *The Old Berkshire Village Book* for this final little anecdote. Apparently in 1852, there were bad floods in the area. So deep was the water that the Great Western train was brought to a halt. Many distinguished passengers had to be rescued by a two-horse farm wagon. Among the eminent evacuees was a chap named Isambard Kingdom Brunel.

KINGHAM

Kingham is the only station on the railway between Stow-on-the-Wold and Chipping Norton. Even so, the line manages to avoid the village by nearly two miles. About 130 years ago, Squire Langston found this gap an inconvenience as it made it difficult for his guests to arrive for his various functions. The squire, being a practical fellow, built a huge hunting lodge beside the station. This building was later transformed into an inn.

The Langston Arms has a ghost or possibly two. In the early 1960s, a slightly luminous Victorian female figure was seen to glide through the premises. The 'Phantom Lady' was witnessed so often in 1964 that the staff took her for granted and hardly glanced up from their work when she appeared. In fact, there were thirty-eight recorded appearances in that year, the Lady appearing punctually on a ten day cycle. There are reports of an attempt at exorcism in 1965 but the clerical gentleman selected for the purpose decided that the spirit was a benign one and refused to banish it from the premises.

There would seem to have been a change of character in the 1970s. A far more alarming spirit took up residence at the pub. The landlord and several of his customers witnessed a shape that expressed a sense of deep depression and fear. It terrorised a barman to such a degree that he was still white and shaking

The Langston Arms, Kingham. (Author's collection)

KIRKLINGTON

There is an unlikely tale here about an old witch who could turn herself into a vixen. The story goes that huntsmen often spotted a fine vixen and gave chase but the animal was far too fleet of foot for them. One day, when they thought they had finally trapped their quarry, the vixen sped into a nearby cottage. A few moments later, the huntsmen, now sure of their prize, burst in through the door. All they could discover within was an old lady, markedly out of breath.

MINSTER LOVELL

The considerable remains of Minster Lovell are as gaunt and forbidding as its story.

There are in fact three haunting tales here. One is brief indeed and concerns an ominous black cloud that hovers over the building, suspiciously like one in the nearby town of Burford (see page 54).

The second Minster Lovell story is shared with Marwell Hall in Hampshire and the Bramshill Police College at Heckfield in the same county. There could be, and probably are, a dozen or more venues throughout the country. Usually referred to as the mistletoe bough, the simple tale varies somewhat according to where one hears it. A pretty young maid (betrothed to a Lovell), is celebrating the night before her wedding. Tired of other amusements, she suggests a game of hide and seek. Being the first to hide, she finds a chest in a seldom used attic. She secrets herself inside, not knowing that the lid is self-locking. The frantic party search for her but she is not found.

> They sought her that night and they sought next day
> They sought in vain while a week passed away.

As in good tradition, Lovell, now grown old, discovers a secret room and the chest, and inside the chest he finds the skeleton of his true love. Minster Lovell has one advantage over the other venues, in so much that it did contain a secret room.

Better authenticated is the story of Francis Lovell, the 9th Baron Lovell. Francis wielded much power, being a favourite of Richard III. It was said at the time that four men ran the country: the King, Sir William Catesby, Sir Ratcliffe and Frances Lovell. A lampoon at the time ran:

> The catte, the ratte and Lovell the dogge
> Rulyth all England under a hogge.

The hog was the King and Lovell had a dog on his crest. Lovell fought for the King at Bosworth, and defeated, he fled to Flanders while his sovereign was killed. He returned to England with 2,000 Yorkist troops to back Lambert Sinnel, a pretender to the throne. They met Henry VII's troops at Stoke and were again soundly beaten. Lovell briefly escaped; he dived into a nearby river but didn't reach the opposite bank.

Henry VIII, a man with a tidy mind, needed to clear up Lovell's property. Although presumed dead, a strong rumour circulated that he had made it back to the hall where he was in hiding. At Henry's convenience, a jury was elected that decided Lovell was dead.

In 1708 the mystery was solved. Four searchers, including a monk, discovered a secret chamber behind an old chimney. There they found the skeleton of a man sitting at a table with a book, paper and pens. In the corner was a cap of Tudor style. There is little doubt that they had found Lord Lovell in his secret chamber. As the discoverers approached, the whole skeleton turned to dust. So, Francis

Minister Lovell Hall, home of the spectral 9th Baron Lovell. (Author's collection)

The ghost of a weeping woman haunts the White Hart, Minster Lovell. (Author's collection)

Lovell had made it back to Minster Lovell and had properly trusted his safety to a servant. Did the servant lose the key? Did he let Francis starve to death? Or did he abscond with considerable family treasures? We shall never know. Obviously, Lovell's spirit was not amused, which is why he has often been sighted bemoaning his fate.

While in Minster Lovell, it is worth taking refreshments at the White Hart. The inn is the home of Rosalind, a far more tempestuous and characterful lady than the previously mentioned Lovell's bride who reputedly haunts the old manor. Rosalind (origin of name unknown) throws glasses, beer mats, occasionally chairs and, once, a handbell. Rosalind also weeps a lot. Could this possibly be because in life she was deserted by her lover? Taking the moral way out of this dilemma, she hanged herself from the stairs.

MURCOTT, NEAR KIDLINGTON

When in the area, a visit to the Nut Tree public house is a must. The pub has a horde of carved gargoyles partially camouflaged in its garden. Suddenly coming across one can be a little surprising, if not alarming. The gargoyles are the work of Canadian sculptor Frederick Close, who left them as a memento of his visit some years ago. The carvings, which are said to be exaggerated models of local characters and patrons, were formerly attached to branches of the pub's walnut tree, but their present abode is pleasant, if disconcerting.

NEWBRIDGE

The Rose Revived stands at Newbridge, which is actually one of the oldest bridges on the Thames, said to date from the 1720s, though parts of it seem even older. It stands near to where the Thames greets her little sister, the Windrush, after they have both meandered their separate ways through Gloucestershire.

This is an inn with a vast, untapped history. Unfortunately, very little has been recorded. On my last visit, a barmaid informed me that the inn has two lady ghosts; a regular one and an occasional one. More information I could not glean.

NORTH LEIGH

There are several strange legends here. Sir William Wilcote and his wife, Lady Elizabeth Blacket (she later remarried) lay in the form of effigies in the chapel at North Leigh. The figures are always known as the Lord and Lady. The Lady has her hands together as if in prayer. Legend dictates that they were once even closer together but are slowly parting. When they are quite apart, Lady Blacket will come back and haunt the village. Another version is that when they part, the

Unusual carvings at the Nut Tree, Murcott. (Author's collection)

Wilcotes will return to search for their buried treasure at nearby Perrott's Hill. They may be disappointed, as an owner of the land in the mid-nineteenth century suddenly became rich.

There is another legendary tale here, which if believed, is a little more frightening. In the nineteenth century, young girls in the village of North Leigh believed that they could attract husbands by going to the churchyard at midnight on Christmas Eve. A ceremony was performed, which included the throwing of hemp seed over their shoulders and reciting:

> Hemp seed I scatter, hemp seed I sow
> He that is my true love, come after me and mow.

Three young girls tried this at the appointed hour. The first girl completed the procedure, which obviously didn't work because she died a spinster in her 80s. The second girl ran screaming that a coffin was chasing her. The third decided that discretion was the better part of valour and remained outside the churchyard. The local elders were sufficiently worried to ban the ceremony from that day on.

ODDINGTON

There is a respectful little grey church at Oddington on the edge of Otmoor. It is strange that it has a repellent rector's brass which depicts a gruesome and horrific skeleton.

Crops are blessed at Oddington on Rogation Sunday and there are several medicinal wells on the sparse moor. The wells are meant to cure a disease in cattle called 'moor evil'. Also the black mysterious water of the peat bogs is said to cure eye and skin complaints.

OTMOOR

This is a bleak expanse of swampy, watery land just east of Oxford. According to legend, an Otmoor Lady once rode around the area of some six square miles while an oat sheaf burned. The understanding was that the ground she circulated would remain common land to be used by the citizens of seven nearby towns.

In the 1980s, Friends of the Earth resisted a motorway being built across the mysterious bleak area by buying tiny pieces of land that would require many expensive compulsory purchase orders.

However, Otmoor was once crossed by a main Roman road from Alchester to Dorchester. The Joseph Stone, still lying beside the track, is thought to have been a Roman milestone.

Oddington Church where engraved in glass is a gruesome skeleton. (Author's collection)

This was not the first time locals had protested; waterlogged it may be, but the locals used to graze sheep and geese there. An attempt was made by the authorities to fence and drain the land in 1830. The locals took offence and broke down the barriers and attacked the workmen. The military were called in. They captured fifty protesters, tied them with heavy ropes and marched them to Oxford city centre. Unfortunately for the authorities, it was St Giles Fair and the place was crowded. Sympathising with the Otmoor people, the crowd attacked the guards and freed the prisoners. No attempt was made to recapture them.

OXFORD

Earth rites and folklore customs
The water from Child's Well at Oxford has the ability to make barren women bring forth children.

On 1 January, each member of Queen's College is presented with a needle threaded with coloured silk and told to take this and be thrifty.

On May Day morning, at 6 a.m., members of Magdalen College go to the top of the 144ft Magdalen Tower and sing hymns and carols; later they dance through the city streets led by local Morris Dancers.

Beating the bounds at Oxford is best described by Reverend Francis Kilvert in 1876, and contained within Roy Christian's *Old English Customs*. The reverend describes how on Ascension Day he was walking with a friend in Merton Gardens. He goes on to describe how they heard excited voices and met a Bachelor and Master of Arts dressed in cap and gown carrying a ladder and accompanied by a group of boys. Each member of the company carried a willow wand with which they beat the old city walls and the terrace walk. Kilvert and friend followed the procession and witnessed the ladder being used for ascending the walls at points where they met the parish bounds. The reverend goes on to report that nearby householders threw sweetmeats for which the young boys scrambled, and at the garden of the President of Corpus, they received their customary bread, ale and cheese. Apparently the little procession was bombarded with water bombs from undergraduates before moving on. At Oriel, there was a grand uproar in the quadrangle as men threw old hats, biscuits and hot coppers. Kilvert described it as a Hogarthian scene before moving to more serene pastures.

Follies
Cauldwell's Castle is next to Folly Bridge, a castellated building with statues set in haphazard profusion. It was built by one of the town's eccentrics in 1849, the accountant Joseph Cauldwell. Cauldwell intended the house to be fortified to afford protection against rioting undergraduates, a perpetual fear of the accountants.

However, it was Cauldwell who proved to be the aggressor after shooting and seriously wounding a student who tried to steal one of his brass cannons.

Another unremarkable folly in Oxford is an early eighteenth-century domed garden house situated behind 16 St Giles Street, previously known as the Judges' Lodging House.

One vote on the town council stopped Oxford from becoming a laughing stock: As recently as 1975, John Madden, an undergraduate, approached the city with plans for the world's largest folly, a 450ft pyramid to be built in Christchurch meadow, apparently with no expense spared. The plan was to freeze over the Thames for seven and a half years in order to excavate the 100ft foundation. It would then take another sixteen and a half years to extract and transport eighteen million tonnes of stone from Headington Quarry. Labour would be no trouble, as a massive army of second-year undergraduates would have a compulsory secondment to sign. It was later discovered that Madden intended to use the structure as his personal mausoleum.

One can hardly believe that the city planners' vote went five to four against the proposal. Possibly the turning point was when it was revealed that the proposed eyesore would plunge the whole city of Oxford into total darkness, thereby necessitating the street lights to be kept on all day.

Heretics and murder
The Martyrs' Memorial in the centre of Oxford commemorates three bishops burned at the stake here in the sixteenth century after Queen Mary's reinstatement of the Catholic faith. The heretics, or Protestant martyrs, were Thomas Cranmer, Archbishop of Canterbury, Nicholas Ridley, Bishop of London, and preacher Hugh Latimer. These were the most notable of the 283 victims of Queen Mary's short and bloody reign. Latimer and Ridley perished horribly in flames at Broad Street. A few months later, the new Bishop Bonner mocked Cranmer and had him dragged in chains through the streets in a ragged nightshirt to his terrible death.

In the thirteenth century, there were many violent clashes in Oxford between the students and townsfolk. After a two-day riot in 1355, the bodies of many students were discovered. The King's Commissioners imprisoned the Mayor and 200 townsfolk. Oxford was run for sometime directly by the Chancellor in London.

Did they hang the wrong man?
Fifty-eight-year-old Alice Louise Kemson was found battered and stabbed to death at Boundary House, St Clements, Oxford on Saturday 1 August 1931.

Alice had intended to stay with a friend in London on 2 August. When she didn't show up, Alice's friend phoned her brother, who lived close by, and asked him to investigate. This he did and came across an horrific scene.

The Martyrs' Memorial, Oxford, where three priests were burned to death

Thomas Cranmer, one of the martyrs to die at Oxford.

The steel band that fastened Cranmer to the stake.

The first thing the police officers tried to establish was the time of death. For some reason the bed was made, curlers were in Alice's hair, breakfast was on the table and, together with the testimony of a shoe salesman, who had tried to make a delivery at 11 a.m. on 1 August and failed, led the police to believe that Alice had met her demise at 10 a.m.

For the next ten days, police interviewed about 300 people. Some had witnessed a travelling salesman selling products door-to-door. He was described as tall with very dark hair. Among items discovered on the premises was a business card in the name of Henry Seymour, who worked for a local firm called Tellus Ltd. Enquiries at Seymour's home address in Oxford showed that the salesman had recently moved to Brighton. Seymour was arrested at Preston Park, Brighton, on 15 August.

In his defence, Seymour claimed that he had stayed at the Greyhound Hotel at Aylesbury from 21–31 July. This was borne out by the Greyhound's landlord, Charles William Parkinson. Seymour admitted to visiting Oxford, along with half a dozen other towns in the vicinity.

At his trial, Seymour claimed that on 31 July, he had missed the last bus back to Aylesbury and stayed at Gypsy Lane with an old customer and friend, Alice Mary Andrews.

Andrews deposed in court that Seymour had arrived at 10.30 p.m. and left at 9.30 a.m. the following morning. She also stated that he had a hammer and a chisel or screwdriver with him. The inference was suggestive to the jury but was not proceeded with greatly by the prosecution. Seymour had caught a bus to Aylesbury at 11 a.m. on 1 August, a fact that was witnessed by a number of passengers. With it being a twenty-two minute walk from Alice Kemson's house, it meant that the latest he could have killed her was 10.38 a.m. Although the evidence against Seymour was fairly strong, it was at best, circumstantial. It would have helped matters if the police had got the right time of death, which they did not.

William Law, who knew Alice, stated that he had seen her on 1 August in Oxford's Pembroke Street at 11.20 a.m. Sarah King, who had known Alice for decades, saw her enter a London bakers at 11.30 a.m. Evelyn Barret, an assistant at the same shop, confirmed the sighting, as she herself had served Alice. A friend of Alice's, a painter by the name of Frederick Taylor, saw her at 12.30 p.m. Taylor deposed that he had known Alice for twenty years. John Woodward, a grocer's assistant, served Alice at 1 p.m. And finally, Kate Barron, who had known Alice all her life, testified that she had waved to Alice near her door at 3 p.m. Amazingly, despite all these testimonies, the jury brought a guilty verdict, though it seems unlikely that six people, with nothing to gain, would have given false evidence.

Justice Swift, (living up to his name), sentenced Seymour to death. At the appeal, incredibly ignoring the six witnesses again, the sentence was upheld. On Thursday 10 December 1931, at Oxford, Henry Daniel Seymour, in all probability an innocent man, took his walk to the scaffold.

The previous story can be found in John J. Eddleston's splendid book, *The Encyclopaedia of Executions*.

In the 1880s, gypsies were not the well-housed and well-heeled people they are today. A large encampment of these people was lodged on wasteland at Cowley. A tent was the nabo hatchin tan (natural living place) of Charles Smith, aged 63, his wife Lucy, who was a couple of years younger and their two teenage children, Prince Albert and Oceana.

Smith was a violent man and gave regular and sound beatings to his wife and offspring. He dispensed his instant justice with a crab-apple stick that was always with him. Living in a tent in the bitter winter of February 1887 could hardly have been conducive with Charles's maintaining a pleasant demeanour.

The family retired to bed on 19 February 1887. Almost at once, brother and sister, heard sounds of violence coming from their parents' bed. Their father was attacking their mother with a hammer. As Oceana ran for help, her brother tried to intervene but it was too late. Lucy Smith crawled from the tent with her skull smashed. She collapsed and died shortly after.

Smith was convicted at Reading. There seemed to be little motive for the crime other than a red-hot violent temper. Smith's plea of insanity was rejected by Baron Huddlestone and he walked to his death on the gallows at Oxford Prison on 9 May 1887.

Mysteries and ghosts
In 1987 at Magdalene College, there were various reports from students who claimed to have seen and heard ghosts in their rooms.

St Peter-in-the-East at Oxford has an underground crypt for the burial of VIPs.

It is not generally known that there was an active printing press in Oxford long before Caxton acquired his in 1477. The Oxford press was designed and operated by a man named Corselus. Other than his name, very little else is known about this gentleman.

Brasenose College actually takes its name from *brasenhuis*, a Dutch word for brew-house, and a brewery once occupied the site. However, students still insist that it comes from a brass nose. The nose has become an emblem and is now incorporated in its coat of arms. There was a brass nose at Stamford where many students, discontented with Oxford, tried to start a new university. When the students returned en masse to Oxford, the emblem remained at Stamford. The students were welcomed back after taking an oath never to lecture or attend lectures at Stamford.

At Queens College on Christmas Day, the ceremony of the boar's head is observed. It is thought to be a Celtic custom as boars were sacred to the Celts. Also, the Norse god Odin was reputed to dine on boar's flesh in Valhalla, the warriors' paradise.

The Provost and Fellows of the College seat themselves at the high table, grace is said, and the college choir follow the boar's head, complete on a silver platter into the room. Three times the procession is halted for a single chorister to sing a verse from the boar's head carol. When the delicacy is finally placed on the table, the soloist receives the orange from the boar's mouth and various other dignitaries are presented with sprigs of bay and rosemary.

On the outskirts of Oxford once stood the Friar Bacon pub. Roger Bacon was a Franciscan monk of the thirteenth century. He was educated far beyond most other men of the age. It was at the Blue Boar Inn (sadly no more) in the city that Friar Bacon lived and did many of his experiments and wrote much of his brilliant philosophy. Roger Bacon had enemies, jealous of his ability. It is rumoured (but never proven) that some conspirators managed to get him imprisoned. Whether or not this is true, Bacon was so ahead of his time that people thought him in league with the Devil, and it was also believed that he practised witchcraft.

The library of St John's College Oxford is inhabited by the ghost of Archbishop Laud, the son of a Reading clothier. He was educated at Oxford and later returned to become Chancellor at St John's. Laud did not die at Oxford; the unfortunate Archbishop was beheaded at the Tower of London in 1645 after being convicted of treason. Laud, who also haunts Hampton Court, seems to be quite a good-humoured old spirit. At St John's, he has been witnessed rolling his head across the floor.

The head-rolling ghost of Archbishop Laud. (B. Allaway)

Friar Roger Bacon was often accused of witchcraft. (B. Allaway)

Oxford inns
The Bear is one of the oldest and possibly most eccentric pubs in Oxford. It is small now, containing only a tiny part of the original hotel that once had thirty bedrooms and stabling for as many horses. The small piece remaining is what was once the ostler's house. In the 1950s, the landlord collected men's neckties. He had some 4,500, most of which are still in situ. Unfortunately, my host no longer gives a free pint to anyone offering a tie.

There are reports of some supernatural occurrences here but nothing first hand or authoritative. I was shown to a cellar where there was a report of a landlord hanging himself. As the ceiling is only 5ft high, he must have been somewhat on the short side.

Although it is in the High Street, the Chequers is difficult to find. It is ancient, believed to date back to 1500. In the seventeenth and eighteenth centuries, the inn exhibited all manner of animal life. It must have been cramped, as the premises once contained, among other animals, several camels, a raccoon and a large fish (type unknown). It was also home to a giant who was popular with students and graced many a dinner table.

There is a rather grim little story attached to the Chequers. During Henry VIII's dissolution of the monasteries, there were numerous priest holes in old inns. The Chequers went further by constructing a tunnel to the Mitre, another ancient hostelry on the other side of the street. If Henry's agents called at either inn, the priests made their way to the hidden passage. Unfortunately, somebody informed about the passage and Henry's men sealed both ends and left the monks inside to starve to death. Occasionally, the chants of dying men can be heard at both the Chequers and the Mitre.

There once was an inn on a main coach road out of Oxford named the Black Drummer. Strange noises were heard in several bedrooms, nothing could be seen, but the sound was similar to pigs scratching and chewing. As trade dropped off, the landlord discovered teeth marks on a leather bottle or saddlebag. Worried about his livelihood, the landlord travelled into Berkshire to seek the help of a cunning man. The first thing the wizard discovered was a neglected graveyard nearby. He soon obtained permission to dig the graveyard up. Among the other badly decayed remains, he found a coffin containing a body that was still covered with flesh. The cunning man ordered the body to be burned, but it would not burn no matter what amount of heat was applied. A college fellow suggested that the cadaver be cut into tiny pieces and fed to the flames bit by bit. The body burned and there were no more strange noises at the inn.

On a lighter note
An Oxford scientist would seem to have perfected the cloning of animals. He took a specialised intestinal cell from a frog and found it had sufficient instructions to

produce a tadpole. The one parent tadpole grew into a frog and the process could be repeated interminably.

Joseph Mellen, who was educated at Oxford and a rowing blue and captain of Oxford University boxing team, was also one of the foremost experimenters of boreholes in the head. (Apparently, opening the skull gave enlightenment to the brain.) Mellen tried to do the operation on himself with a type of brace and bit. Mellen asked assistance of Amanda Fielding, another borehole experimentalist. Together they managed to get a spike to grip onto Joseph's skull and started cranking the saw. However, Mellen fainted and Amanda called an ambulance. On a third attempt, Mellen was lucky to survive. A fourth attempt in which Mellen operated on himself would seem to have been successful. He claimed to have reached a state of freedom and serenity that stayed with him for the rest of his life. Joseph convinced Amanda to follow his lead. She performed her own trepanation while Mellen recorded the event with a cine camera. The operation was a success and the pair, now a family, seem to have had a joyous existence ever since.

An advertisement in an Oxford newspaper brought many celebrated dons to a lecture by Dr Emil Busch. Dr Busch was a bohemian type with a long beard. He had a deep guttural German accent and much that he said was lost on the audience. This was hardly surprising as it was later revealed that Busch was actually an undergraduate and his lecture was complete gibberish.

The fair at Walton (now part of Oxford), really a wake, is one of the largest survivors of patronal fairs. St Giles Fair at Oxford has outlived the city's four Charter Fairs. Its original site was at St Giles and Magdalen Street and was in the manor of Walton outside the city walls.

The story goes that the trouble between university and town came about when a student became very friendly with a local tradesman's daughter. The student, reputedly by the name of Fox, discovered he had impregnated the girl. To talk it over, he arranged to meet his beloved in a field outside town (now very much inside town). The girl, no fool, arrived early and hid herself in a tree. She was a little surprised when her lover arrived and started digging a grave. The lady did not reveal herself until her beloved had finished his grisly task, got fed up with waiting and returned to his college. Legend dictates that when he called at her father's house the following morning, he was greeted by the maiden who waxed lyrical:

> One moonshiny night, as I sat high
> Waiting for one to come by
> The boughs did bend, my heart did ache
> To see the hole Fox did make.

Her wit cost her her life. The student lost his temper and stabbed her to death on the doorstep. This caused violent and fatal battles between town and gown. It is said that Brewers Lane ran red with blood. The student buried his lover in the already prepared grave, which is said to be at Divinity Walk.

After an extensive tour of strange Oxford, a drink is called for. At the Horse and Jockey in Woodstock Road, there is an extraordinary assortment of bizarre and grotesque furnishings and decor. There are walls and ceilings covered with newspapers, outsize games, a sawn-off metal bath standing against the wall and the portrait of a strange woman who seems to be climbing out of the frame. The list could go on for some time, but it is a pub that is best to experience in person.

One should really not leave Oxford without visiting the city's Pitt Rivers Museum. It is as colourful and unique as it is little known. It stands behind the Oxford University Museum of Natural History and could take at least a week to fully walk around its entirety. Lieutenant General Augustus Henry Lane Fox Pitt Rivers started his collection in the mid-nineteenth century. Several floors contain overfilled cabinets and drawers overflowing with every describable artefact, curio, trinket, novelty, bibelot and knick-knack from every conceivable country of the world. The collection, described very loosely as anthropological, must run into many hundreds of thousands of items, and includes such objects as betel chewing gum, tongue scrapers, sharks' teeth and whistling arrowheads. It would take a complete volume to describe the Pitt Rivers collection, but one thing you should not dream of going out without seeing is the massive collection of artefacts designed to wield off the evil eye.

Oxford tail pieces
Did you know that in 1898, Oxford witnessed the first commercial traveller to use a car? Ralph Foort, the driver, was a native of the town. The town also employed the first lollipop lady.

Both King Richard and his brother King John were born in the city. The Lionheart saw the light of day at what is now 24 Beaumont Street.

Frank Cooper's marmalade has been made in Oxford since the 1870s. It was surplus from Cooper's supply for his own consumption and was made from a recipe handed down to his wife, Sarah Jane, by her mother. Its popularity soon increased and long queues formed outside Cooper's shop. Robert Scott took a jar to Antarctica, where it was discovered in the snow many years later. These above three entries can be found in Christopher Winn's *I Never Knew That about England*.

Here is a great ghoul to finish the report on Oxford. 'Boneless' is without doubt the most hideous and disgusting spectre of all and haunts the rural paths of the county. 'Boneless' is well named. It is a large lump of white decaying flesh that wobbles across remote parts like a gigantic jelly. Although it is limbless, it is reported to move at incredible speed when giving chase. It exudes an extremely putrid aroma when smothering and then engulfing its hapless human victims.

Richard the Lionheart and his brother John were both born in Oxford.

RADLEY

On Easter Sunday, the people of Radley go through a ceremony known as 'clipping the church'. It seems this ancient custom requires parishioners to embrace the church by joining hands round it in the form of dance.

RYCOTE CHAPEL ALBURY

Rycote Chapel, this unique building, was constructed in 1449 by Richard Quatermain and his wife Sibill. It has been described as a perfect gem of Perpendicular interior architecture. This wonderful little structure, which is externally embellished with the original fifteenth-century pinnacles and battlements, was once adjoined to a mighty Tudor manor house named Rycote Park. Unfortunately, much of the building was destroyed by fire in the eighteenth century, leaving St Michael's, the chapel, to stand alone.

After the death of Quatermain (sometimes Quatermaynes), Rycote Park passed into the hands of Sir Richard Fowler, a man famous for his imprudent spending. Unfortunately for Fowler, he managed to marry two successive women, both of whom shared his penchant for lavish entertaining. The outcome of this was that in 1521, he was forced to sell his magnificent home.

The new owner was one John Heron, whose son Giles married Cicely, the youngest daughter of Sir Thomas More. Sir Thomas paid many visits to his daughter at the home she loved so dearly. But history relates that both he and Giles Heron fell foul of Henry VIII and were soon beheaded, leaving Cicely to stand on her own.

The manor house's next owner was Lord Williams of Thame. It was used by Henry VIII and his new bride, Catherine Howard, for their honeymoon. A few short months later, Catherine was beheaded.

Sir John Williams was an honoured and very wealthy man. He was master of the Royal Jewels and Henry's right-hand man, which was a very good way of surviving; being a leading figure in the dissolution of the monasteries did his standing, and his pocket, no harm.

Later, when Queen Mary married Philip of Spain, Lord Williams was made Lord Chamberlain and was greatly involved in the burning of Bishops Cranmer, Latimer, and Ridley. Although placed as a guard to Princess Elizabeth, whom he held under house arrest, he seems to have been forgiven when she finally succeeded her father to the throne. After Lord William's death, skulduggery continued at Rycote. His daughter survived him and married Henry Norreys, whose father was accused of criminal complicity with Anne Boleyn. They were both executed at the Tower.

One of Elizabeth I's companions when she visited Rycote was Robert Dudley, a dangerous man greatly suspected of the murder of his wife Amy Robsart (see page 57). The owner, now Lady Norreys, disliked Dudley so much that she made him sleep in the stables. Shortly after, he was to die after receiving a threat from the ghost of Amy Robsart.

When James I came to the throne, Francis Norreys, grandson of the first Henry Norreys, inherited Rycote. After years of debauchery, he finally committed suicide by shooting himself with his crossbow in the park. It would seem that although it was beautiful, Rycote was not a particularly lucky place.

The house was inherited by his daughter and later by her grandson, the Earl of Abingdon. Sadly, in 1745, the house caught fire, killing his 10-year-old son. Much of the building material that was left was used for buildings in local villages. Many years later, the house was tastefully restored. However, little now remains.

The chapel has four ghosts. The more famous are Robert Dudley, Earl of Leicester, and Sir Thomas More, who often prayed devoutly here. There is also a brown monk, who seems to be the most prevalent of the four and has been seen more than a dozen times in fairly recent history. He has no name and one wonders why it is one particular monk and not one of several that remain; he has been seen at different times in different places. During the Second World War, when the house became a hospital for children, the brown friar was reported on many occasions. It is not thought that this could be put down to vivid childhood imagination as the children knew nothing of the monk when the story was related to them. But in time they came to accept him. It has been suggested that the brown friar was slain during Henry VIII's dissolution of the monasteries but all is supposition.

Rycote Park chapel, home to a variety of ghosts.

There is also a grey lady at Rycote Chapel named Arabella, though why, no one knows. She is silent, devout and crosses the chapel in peaceful serenity before departing through a wall that once held a door to the old house. Several people who have seen Arabella describe her as being attired in Tudor dress and the more informed think that Arabella is far more likely to be Cicely, the demure lady who loved the place above all others, though why the name was changed is not known. This is a place where all four ghosts cohabit in friendly, peaceful tranquillity.

SHILTON

Shilton is an attractive hamlet surrounded by bare and noble hills. The tiny River Shill, from which the village takes its name, runs among the pleasant and ancient houses. The river, however, is a mixed blessing as it is said to be responsible for Shilton's nickname 'Silly Shilton'. It is rumoured that the village received its unenviable prefix because locals had a habit of herding fish under a small stone bridge called the Arch every time it rained, presumably to keep them dry.

A second tale of Shiltonians is that they once tried to rake the reflection of a full moon out of the water, thinking it to was a round cheese.

I have heard the latter on numerous occasions, but usually attached to villages in Wiltshire. In most cases, the locals had secreted contraband in the village pond. To escape detection when the revenue men approached, they grabbed rakes and explained that they were trying to catch a cheese. Creased with laughter, the revenue men continued on their way, thinking it a village totally populated by idiots. Hence, Wiltshire people being known as Moonrakers.

'Silly Shilton'. (Author's collection)

SHIPTON-UNDER-WYCHWOOD

A mysterious old area is the Wychwood Forest. Shipton is a pleasant village with a green surrounded by chestnut trees. In their shade is a gabled fountain which commemorates seventeen local men who died in 1874. The men, together with hundreds more people, were heading to New Zealand in the *Cospatrick*. Just off Tristan Da Cunha, fire broke out and up to 500 people perished at sea.

Close to the memorial stands the ancient Shaven Crown inn. The old hostelry was built by the monks of Bruern Abbey and served as a hostelry for travellers to the monastery until the abbey became yet another victim of the dissolution. The inn survives with its perfect Perpendicular fourteenth-century gateway and its stoned courtyard. However, the name, the Shaven Crown, is a fairly modern invention. It did not arrive until 1927 and in all probability, refers to a monk's tonsure. As far as I know, there are no resident ghosts at the Shaven Crown, but nearby Shipton Court, surrounded with its beautiful gardens and ornamental lake, once had a very hostile poltergeist. It was such trouble that a form of exorcism was performed. Having backed the unquiet spirit into a room, the entrance was swiftly sealed. Unfortunately for would-be ghost hunters, it is unknown where the room and its spirited occupant are actually situated.

There is one more little tale before leaving Shipton. There is reported to be an underground passage from Bruern to Tangley Hall, some four miles away. From

The Shaven Crown, Shipton-under-Wychwood. (Author's collection)

time to time, a spectral monk has been witnessed traversing the paths that run parallel to the tunnel.

STANTON HARCOURT

Stanton Harcourt's quoits sadly are no longer in situ. They were removed during the Second World War to make way for an airfield. The Devil's Quoits were so called because, when Old Nick was playing quoits on a Sunday, he was asked to desist. In temper, he threw the three massive stones towards the river but they landed in a field at Stanton Harcourt.

SWINBROOK

Swinbrook is a pleasant little Cotswold village with homely cottages where the babbling Windrush winds its way through the meadows. This was once the home of the Fettiplace family, once thought to be, in Tudor and Stuart times, the richest family in England. It is known for a fact that they had large properties in fifteen counties. In 1503, Fettiplace built a house at Swinbrook which was described by writers of the time as a palace, one of the finest houses in the country. All has now gone; not a stone remains.

The Fettiplaces did little to distinguish themselves in war or peace. Their one talent was for making money, with which they were chiefly absorbed. To give credit where it is due, the Fettiplaces started many charities, the offspring of which are still in existence today. They also erected an extremely beautiful church, which included in the chancel six effigies of family members, complete with their coats of arms.

The Fettiplaces not only haunt the church but also the vicarage. A kneeling figure, armed and armoured, has been witnessed in the chancel. His identity is unknown but there is a strong suggestion that this is Sir John Fettiplace. Sir John died suddenly and was suspected of being poisoned by his wife Susanna, who found her husband a dull fellow. Charges were brought against her but were dropped through lack of evidence. Shortly after her acquittal, Susanna teamed up with a handsome young blade named Sir Thomas Cutler and took off for Lechlade.

Another candidate for the kneeling ghost is Sir George Fettiplace, whose smiling bust looks down in the chancel. It is said that exception proves the rule. If so, Sir George, the last male of the line, fits the exception of the staid Fettiplaces. He loved gambling, cock-fighting, horse racing, women, drinking and wholesale debauchery. George died suddenly from a heart attack after a violent quarrel at the Bull in Burford.

Keith B. Poole's *Ghosts of Wessex* contains detailed information concerning the vicarage at Swinbrook. The book describes a whole host of unusual events;

footsteps which had been heard running on the stairs, doors opening and closing; and a tiny bevelled cradle that rocked alone. The family's dogs barked, growled and shook. They also refused bluntly to go upstairs, for there, in a bedroom, a spectre was actually seen and an icy atmosphere had settled on the bed. There would seem to be a variety of supernatural events at the vicarage, but nobody who has experienced them has ever described a feeling of malice. Earthly and spectral inhabitants seem to accept this sort of benign cohabitation.

Before leaving Swinbrook, the Fettiplaces and their doomed palatial manor, we must have a brief word about a man named Freeman. After Sir George's demise, a tenant was found for the manor in the shape of Mr Freeman. He was popular with the locals due to his wit, generosity and lavish lifestyle. Villagers were often guests at his home. This was the time of horse-drawn coaches, footpads and highwaymen which were the plague of the roads, the main London to Gloucester road being no exception. Imagine their surprise when a gang of highwaymen were ambushed one night. Several were wounded and taken into custody, among them the charismatic Mr Freeman of stately Swinbrook Manor. Freeman found his way to the gallows and the splendid manor fell into disrepair and was finally demolished.

TACKLEY

Beside the Oxford to Banbury road at Tackley stands an inn named Sturdy's Castle. The sign portrays two combatants locked in an enraged battle. Legend dictates that the two protagonists were named Sturdy and Castle and that they fought to the death here. The cause is unknown but it was probably over land ownership. Sturdy is reputed to have slain Castle and then, ironically, lost his life – he was hanged on the spot.

I was informed that in the 1960s, the water at the inn was still supplied by wells fed by local streams. Also, for some reason that I have been unable to discover, Sturdy's Castle was known as the Spud Pub.

THAME

Thame is an ancient, tranquil and dignified little town. It was here in 1643 that John Hampden died after nearly a week of suffering, having been fatally wounded at Chalgrove Field. It was here that the famous opposition leader attended school. The school is also associated with Dr Fell, Dean of Christ Church and the man who thought education could be flogged into scholars. Hence the famous nursery rhyme, *I do not like thee Dr Fell.*

Sturdy's Castle inn sign at Tackley. (Author's collection)

The most striking and famous building in Thame is the Bird Cage Inn. Dating from the fifteenth century, it is most people's archetypal idea of what an old world inn should be. Although the building has been through several architectural changes from its original form, there is plenty of the old building remaining to be of interest. The vast and pleasantly distorted beams, the twisted projecting timbers and the elegant original windows are reminiscent of Walt Disney – a fairytale creation deposited in an Oxfordshire market town.

As one would expect, the Bird Cage's past is colourful and a little dubious. The vast cellar was once used as a staging prison for French troops during the Napoleonic Wars. A whipping post and stocks stood directly outside to encourage the inmates to behave. Up until this time, the inn was known as the Blackbird, but after it became the unwelcome quarters of the French, it became the Bird and Cage; then through a logical progression to 'The Bird Cage'.

If the enforced guests in the cellars were unhappy with their lot, they were infinitely better off than the inhabitants of the top floor of the building. There, cramped and crowded in a small room, was a colony of lepers. Leprosy was the scourge of Britain for nearly three centuries. The disease was believed to be far more contagious than it actually was, and those suffering from it were forced to wear a form of cowbell and roam the countryside begging food from those brave enough to approach them.

Some authorities, such as Thame, took a slightly more enlightened view and permitted their local lepers to remain in town, albeit in a much restricted area. The Bird Cage was chosen probably for its height and because its captive audience below could hardly complain. The lepers were locked in a tiny room to await approaching death, but were sustained by food and water passed in through a trapdoor on long poles, a job that fell to the brothers of a nearby monastery.

A story based more on speculation is that of a young leper, sick and tired of being restricted, who escaped through the trapdoor and ran through the town. The appalling disfigurement of the young man shocked the populace into action. Stones were thrown at the horribly deformed leper until he sat in the town centre, head in hands, bleeding profusely. More and more stones rained down on the poor man's head until finally he fled back to his sanctuary at the top of the Bird Cage Inn, only to die from his wounds later that evening.

Apparently, it is this unfortunate young man that is the unrested spirit at the inn. The paranormal phenomena at the Bird Cage have been occurring for a number of years and are quite well attested.

A couple that took over the inn in the late 1960s experienced a cold and oppressive atmosphere in one of the second floor rooms, as well as knocking. These strange encounters began to endanger the landlady's health and, after discussing the matter with regulars, the Society for Psychical Research was contacted. They turned up in force and after some days of diligence, the society members detected, or rather experienced, a loud and violent knocking. They managed to ascertain that the disturbance was indeed instigated by the sorrowful leper. A communication system was set up with a simplified Morse code arrangement. A question would be asked and the restless spirit would answer with one knock for the affirmative and two for a negative reply. After hours of this labour intensive interview, investigators were able to interpret that the young man had been stoned to death, that he was an atheist, and that he hated people in general and wished to be left alone.

The phantom's wishes, however, went unheeded, for the investigators returned on several occasions. Contact being made, they found the spirit far more annoyed and irritated by the intrusion into his privacy. The questions were answered by such hostile phrases as, 'Leave me alone or I'll kill you'.

Once again his appeals were unheeded; in fact, his privacy was to be invaded to an even greater extent by a film crew, hoping to do a programme on the paranormal. According to some reports, the sound engineer had a variety of troubles with his equipment, from the trivial annoyance of a plug being pulled from a socket to a severe or total malfunction of his complete electrical apparatus. All he had been able to record were three words: 'leave me alone'.

The Birdcage Inn, Thame, has a very checkered past. (Author's collection)

The spectral leper of the Birdcage Inn, Thame. (Author's collection)

How much credence the reader puts on this report is entirely a matter of individual conjecture, and like all good stories, it may encourage embellishment as it is retold.

There is, however, a strange rejoinder to the above statement. Sometime after the investigation, the landlady was in conversation with a verbose disbeliever in the bar; during the discussion, a small mug seemed to take off from its hook and, of its own volition, fly across the bar towards the sceptic. Unfortunately, the landlady chose this moment to alter her position and was struck on the back of her neck. Was it a coincidence, and if not, who was the intended target – the converted or the critic?

WESTON ON THE GREEN

This is an idyllic village on the Oxford to Bicester road. There are three supernatural spirits at the Western Manor Hotel. The road outside the hotel, which is thought to have led to a monastery, is haunted by a phantom coach and horses. Not often witnessed nowadays with the invention of the petrol engine, the coach was once thought to have left the main road here and clatter into the hotel's courtyard and stables.

Another ghost seldom seen is that of a dairymaid, who was found dying in the yard after a suicide leap from a tower.

Probably the most famous ghost here is that of Mad Maude, thought to have been an attractive but simple-minded peasant girl who was the play-thing of the lustful monks. Maude was unfortunately foolish enough to talk about her transgressions. She was accused of witchcraft by the monks, who claimed to have been bewitched by her, and was burned at the stake. It is alleged that she haunts the Oak Room at the hotel.

WILCOTE

This is an attractive village situated in Oxford's somewhat eerie Wychwood Forest. This is one of the few villages in the south that still performs 'well ceremonies'. On Palm Sunday, children repair to Lady's Well where they mix liquorice with well water.

The mad and bad Sir William and Lady Wilcote haunt nearby North Leigh, but are not averse to making the odd appearance at Wilcote. Lord Wilcote had a habit, after his death, of ringing the church bell here; the rector, who could not sleep, bravely got up to question the ghost. Lord Wilcote pointed out that he could not rest peacefully in his grave while the bell was being tolled. He suggested that the rector remove the clapper and cast it into a nearby pond.

There are varying stories as to whether the spectral Lord's wish was granted. One tale has a dozen priests trying to lay to rest this sprightly ghost, who taunts them, saying that he will haunt them while the clapper and bell stay together. In some versions, the priests grant his wishes, throwing the clapper into a pond and burying the bell in the woods. Other reports have the bad Lord transmuting into a ghostly black dog. There was some sort of ceremony performed here at the birth of a newborn baby. Two bell clappers were thrown into separate ponds, the belief being that if they returned together, the black dog (Sir William) would reappear.

WITNEY

There must be a hundred strange tales of this lovely old town, but I could find very little indeed.

The Rowing Machine Inn, although close to the Little Windrush, has nothing to do with the river. A rowing machine was a contraption used in the manufacture of the town's world famous blankets, a horse-operated machine that was used for raising the pile. There are illustrations and memorabilia in the pub. The man who watched the horse must have had a job that made him incredibly thirsty. A bill from the blanket mill dated 1782 informs us that he consumed 196 pints at a cost of $22s\ 8d$.

Before leaving the attractive old town of Witney, do make a trip to the Boot Inn. The landlord has made an extremely fascinating collection of famous footwear. Many of the shoes and boots have been donated by celebrities. Sporting footwear from George Best, Jeremy Clarkson and Geoff Hurst stand smartly labelled next to shoes of such showbiz stars as Clive James and Ronnie Barker. Well worth a visit.

WOODSTOCK

The history of Woodstock predates Blenheim Palace. This attractive little town on the River Glyme is mentioned in the Domesday Book. Blenheim now stands on the site of Woodstock Manor House and was the birthplace of the Black Prince in 1331. An inscribed stone on Blenheim Palace Bridge testifies to this fact. Less well known is Blenheim's Fair Rosamund's Well, that was once reputed to have healing waters. Woodstock Manor House was destroyed in 1649 during the Civil War, but not before Cromwell's Parliamentarian commissioners who resided here had experienced the actions of an animated poltergeist. Nicknamed 'the Royalist Devil of Woodstock', the poltergeist made a regular habit of moving beds with great ferocity, blowing out candles, throwing glasses at the wall and drenching

The Bear Hotel, Woodstock. (Author's collection)

the servants in stinking water. Little wonder the Royal Commission moved to other premises, leaving the manor to the Royal Devil and a spectral black dog that also frequented the premises.

Blenheim Palace also has a ghost, reputed to be Dean Jones, chaplain to the 1st Duke of Marlborough. The Dean haunts a couple of corridors and the room where Winston Churchill was born. Known as the Black Ghost because of his clerical garb, the spectral Dean allegedly searches for a book that he loaned to the first Duchess of Marlborough.

Back in town stands the Bear, a delightful old coaching inn that boasts that it was old when Blenheim was new. Old it certainly is – parts of it date back to 1232. However, most of the structure goes back to the sixteenth or seventeenth century.

It was in the sixteenth century that the old inn witnessed one of its murders, a woman reputedly strangled in the cellar. A second slaying came in the seventeenth century, when a servant girl secretly gave birth to a child and stuffed it in the chimney for fear of discovery.

Whether or not the above ladies are responsible for the reported supernatural happenings at the inn is unknown. Hilary Rice in her *Ghosts of the Chilterns and Thames Valley* informs us of an occurrence in 1976 when a party of guests were still in fine form in the bar at 2.30 a.m. At 2.40 a.m., a lady left the room to go

Blenheim Palace, Woodstock.

upstairs, she returned screaming that she had met a ghostly lady on the landing. The night porter went to investigate but discovered very little except an extremely cold patch where the spirit had been seen, which seemed strange on such an extremely muggy night. There have also been reports of locked and latched doors being opened, and some Americans noticed a peculiar and eerie shadow.

From other sources I have gleaned that, quite recently, the Bear has been inflicted with some mild poltergeist activity which would seem to involve light switches, the opening of drawers and footsteps in empty corridors. Room 16 seems to be the most affected.

There has long been disagreement among scholars as to where Henry II's mistress, Fair Rosamund, met her death. It was probably at Godstow or Woodstock, though there are a couple of other lesser contenders.

Woodstock claims that Henry built a vast house here. Whether or not this is the destroyed Woodstock Manor is another bone of contention. Henry instructed his builders to fashion a large maze around the house, which could only be fathomed by him and Rosamund, thereby securing her safety. Unfortunately for the pair, Queen Eleanor found her way through and offered her husband's mistress the dagger or the poisoned chalice. The Fair Rosamund chose the latter.

It may be wondered how the slighted Queen found her way through the maze. Raphael Holinshed in his *Chronicles* of 1577 suggests that when leaving his mistress's room, a thread from his sock got caught and unwound, unwittingly showing his wife the way through the maze.

YARNTON

On the first Monday after St Peter' Day, 29 June, the mowing rights for certain meadows are drawn by lots, represented by large wooden balls. The mowing rights of Pixey Mead and West Mead are offered for sale at the Grapes Inn. The thirteen mead balls are then drawn, which are inscribed with the names of the original eleventh century tenant farmers.

3

NORTH OXFORDSHIRE

ADDERBURY

It is presumed that Sir George Cobb is the occupant of the phantom coach and horses that's said to appear at Adderbury Green. The spectre of the coach appears on a dark night with its black horses breathing fire from their nostrils, speeding across parkland where Cobb House once stood.

Sir George was a brave man, and death held little fear for him when he met it in 1762, but his restful spirit was disturbed when four oak trees were felled some years later. The destroying of these trees was a direct contravention of his deathbed orders. The phantom coach appeared shortly after; first witnessed by a pair of poachers, and has been attested to on several occasions since.

If poor old Sir George's spirit was troubled by the loss of the trees, his wrath must have been extreme when the old house was demolished in the nineteenth century.

It is alleged that the Devil was keen to have a church at Adderbury and Bloxham. Legend dictates that the two brothers who constructed the buildings employed an itinerant mason who worked at a ferocious pace and without pay. The contract was completed in a very short time and the mason disappeared, leaving behind a cloven footprint and a distinct and worrying whiff of sulphur.

In no way conflicting with the Devil theory are some of the sculptures and illustrations in or upon Adderbury's church. As they are similar to those described at Bloxham (*see* page 107), I shall not go into too much detail here. However, I shall mention one which shows details of an archer who took aim at a slinking creature and badly missed. The arrow came to rest in an old woman's knee, leaving her in pain and terror and hanging onto her cow's neck for support. There are also some heinous-looking corbels on the church wall gazing down with malevolence.

Adderbury Church. (Author's collection)

ALKERTON

There is very little of the unusual to report about this hillside-clinging little village, other than it is one of the four villages that the imaginative and somewhat bizarre Masonic brothers built. Their endeavours are sufficiently described in the other three: Adderbury, Bloxham and Hanwell.

Here at Alkerton, the masons and their cloven-hoofed employee seem to have restricted themselves to portraying an archer, a harpist, an organist, a muzzled bear and a scattering of dogs.

The fine Jacobean rectory here was constructed by the rector himself, Thomas Lydyat, the son of the lord of the manor. Lydyat became famous for his writings throughout Europe. He was also renowned for his prolific studies of astronomy and chronology. This endeared Lydyat to Charles Stuart's brother, Henry, whose tutor he became.

Lydyat's father gave him the living of Alkerton where he carried on writing. Unfortunately, he had pledged to cover the debts of a prodigal brother, which he was unable to do, so Thomas was cast into prison. Gaol in those days was far from pleasant and shortly after his release in 1646, Lydyat died of a condition almost certainly brought about by his incarceration. All his works have now been forgotten but Lydyat is briefly mentioned in a poem by Dr Johnson.

BANBURY

The Reindeer Inn at Banbury was once haunted by a grim Cavalier; this particular ghost exuded a feeling of foreboding and inexplicable dread. The spirit is thought to be one of the Cavaliers that was tried and sentenced by Parliamentarian forces in the Reindeer's famous Globe Room.

The apparition ceased when Banbury Council bought the decorative ceiling and panelling of the Globe Room. The Town Hall was the new recipient of the materials, but there is no evidence of the foreboding Cavalier following his surroundings. When I visited the Reindeer in 2007, much of the panelling had been returned.

The faint sighting of a spirit at Tadmarten Heath near Banbury is thought to have brought about the deranged and contagious euphoria that took place in the area.

A strange gathering of people assembled on the hill in the late 1960s and tried to raise the spirit of Will Blackhall – a gypsy hangman. The group held hands and chanted, and while plentiful cine-cameras were poised, nothing materialised.

Not the proudest of Banbury's boasts is that in the seventeenth century, it possessed an underground cell with an open sewer running through it. A Quaker, Anne Audland, who was chained there, was all but smothered by toads and frogs.

The Reindeer Inn, Banbury, home to the ghostly Cavalier. (Author's collection)

Over the centuries, practically anything of historical interest seems to have been destroyed in Banbury. In the seventeenth century, the citizens petitioned Parliament to pull down their vast castle to use the masonry to repair the town after the Civil War. In the eighteenth century, citizens blew up their beautiful old church rather than restore it. An upsurge of Puritanism three centuries ago also destroyed the original cross; the cross seen today was erected in 1859.

Although Lady Godiva and Queen Elizabeth I have been suggested, 'The Fine Lady' is thought to have been a member of the Fiennes family from Broughton Castle, and the 'ride on the cock horse', as we know it from the nursery rhyme, would have probably been part of the May Day celebrations.

What isn't generally known is that Dean Swift took the name Gulliver for the hero of *Gulliver's Travels* from a gravestone in Banbury's churchyard.

Banbury, which is at the centre of several ley lines, has been the subject of many UFO sightings over the past fifty years.

Banbury's famous cross. (Author's collection)

Banbury's Fine Lady. (Author's collection)

Jonathan Swift, who obtained the unusual name for his hero Gulliver from a gravestone in Banbury's churchyard.
(B. Allaway)

The grave of a man named Gulliver, Banbury. (Author's collection)

The Cromwell Lodge Hotel is thought to be haunted, though not by some fatally wounded Ironside seeking refuge after a blood shedding battle but by a mischievous child, a little girl who exasperatingly hides various items. I enquired of one of the staff about this playful spirit. She admitted the existence of this frolicsome and pernicious imp but would not be drawn in. She pointed out that she 'lived in' and did not wish to incur the spook's displeasure.

Kelly, a barmaid at the Three Pigeons, was far more forthcoming about the establishment's meddlesome ghost. The pub, dating from around 1648, rivals the Reindeer as the oldest in town. The spirit has a liking for spirits of the alcoholic variety and regularly empties the optics. It also moves glasses around in mid-air.

BARFORD ST JOHN

Barford St John lies on the slopes of a valley gazing across the stripling River Swere to its sister village, Barford St Michael. A farmhouse below has fragments of a window, which, apart from the traces of the moat, is all that is left of the castle here, the history of which seems to be completely unknown.

The Cromwell, home to the spirit of a playful little girl. (Author's collection)

The Three Pigeons, Banbury, is home to a thirsty ghost. (Author's collection)

BLOXHAM

Bloxham is a famous and attractive village. Its mighty church tower is 200ft high and is arguably the loftiest in the county. The building originated in Norman times but there has been much development since.

On the internal walls, one may observe Christ in Judgement and also with his disciples. But the church is mentioned in this volume because of other strange depictions, perhaps not so strange if one considers the other nearby churches, Addebury, Alkerton and Hanwell, built by the fourteenth-century masons.

The peculiar designs include a dragon swallowing lost souls, a monkey running off with a jug, men playing harps, a fiddler and a couple of crowned heads. Entertainingly; a fox is depicted making away with a goose, hotly pursued by a farmer with a cudgel and his wife with her distaff following.

If these pictures seem strange, those in the cornice of the north aisle seem almost cartoon-like. We have two monkeys riding on a cat; a man blowing a horn; a pair of hounds looking for a rabbit that is crouching in the thicket; and farmyard scenes including a pheasant, a cockerel and a large pig complete with seven piglets. There are also two gentlemen armed with swords and shields about to do battle, and a man with a strange creature on his back, or a sack, or even possibly a set of bagpipes. I was also told there is a whistling man among the characters but I could not find him, unless he is the unpleasant, unnerving creature that greets one from the porch.

Strange corbels at Bloxham Church. (Author's collection)

A strange greeting at Bloxham Church.

C.J. Wilson was reputed to have been the first border at the famous Bloxham School. He arrived in 1860 as a pupil and stayed on as a master for decades. On retirement from teaching, he took up the post of secretary for the Old Boys' Society until he finally retired in 1937, unfortunately dying two years later at the age of 91. Wilson had spent an incredible seventy-seven years at the same location. He was also thought to have been the inspiration for H.G. Wells' *Goodbye Mr Chips*.

An intriguing article by Tim Healey in the magazine *Oxfordshire* contains information on Bloxham's underground system of caves, an assortment of tunnels running under Bloxham from varying times and for varying purposes. The longest and most ambitious is reputed to run from the village to Broughton Castle, though there seems to be very little evidence of its existence.

What is known is that there exists a cave or tunnel that was documented in 1825 by Harry Davis, the Bloxham vicar's son. Davis describes how some workmen had inadvertently exposed an opening, which in turn had revealed a collection of spears and battleaxes thought to be the weapons of ancient warriors. Black ashes

C.J. Wilson of Bloxham school is thought to have been the model for Mr Chips. (B. Allaway)

that were found with the weapons were presumed to be the remains of these noble champions. Sadly, later excavations suggested that the ashes were coal dust.

In 1902, Healey informs us that once again, the tunnel was accidentally exposed, this time by a road roller. The local schoolmaster seized the opportunity for exploration by sending down his pupils, strung in a line by a cord and bearing candles. Nothing seems to be recorded as to what, if anything, was discovered.

The third exposure came in 1954, this time in conjunction with sewerage works. Even in those enlightened days, it seems that it was difficult to tell what was man-made and what was caused by natural water erosion. There was talk of nineteenth-century ironstone mines and a tunnel thought to lead from Queens Street to nearby Ashwell House. There is a story that goes some way in support of this theory. Apparently, the lady owner of Ashwell House discovered that her boot boy had been exploring from her end and had the tunnel closed forthwith.

Yet another blocked-off tunnel is reputed to run from the seventeenth-century Hawk and Partridge Inn to nearby St Mary's Church. It was discovered in 1920 and soon acquired the mawkish nickname of Bodysnatchers Lane. Even if it was not designed for the purpose, it would have been a godsend to any resurrectionists. A local man in 1905 reported that his grandfather and two workmates chased away some resurrectionists with scythes.

Finally in 1890, Mr Healey informs us that a local sexton was reopening a grave in the churchyard and promptly fell into a tunnel. This time it was reputed to lead to Godswell House, a place of pilgrimage. Naturally, locals perceived it to be a body snatchers' tunnel. Could it possibly have been where a previous grave once was?

Today, the Hawk and Partridge is now a private residence and should be respected as such.

CHASTLETON

Not to be outdone by Claydon, Chastleton has a stone, (admittedly two miles away from the village) that denotes where four counties meet.

Chastleton House, said to be built on an ancient earthwork, is a Jacobean construction designed by Walter Jones in 1603. The grounds were given a unique formation with their splendid yews cut to resemble rabbits, cats, dogs, baskets, armchairs, teapots and even old men. There was a previous building here that was sold by Robert Gatesby in 1601. Gatesby was an English conspirator who was the son of William Gatesby of Ladworth, Warwickshire. As a Catholic, William had suffered much under Queen Elizabeth I and was heavily fined for his part in the Essex Rebellion. This embittered Robert to the extent that he was one of the main instigators of the gunpowder plot. The downfall of this project is well known. When Fawkes was arrested, Gatesby and his fellow conspirators fled. On

7 November 1605, Gatesby and some of his crew were surrounded in Holbeach House. A siege followed and Gatesby was killed by a bullet. A rumour insists that Gatesby, covered in blood, crawled across the floor to kiss a picture of the Virgin Mary, his final act.

There is a secret chamber in Charleston House in what is known as the Cavaliers' room. The story goes that after the Battle of Worcester, Charleston's owner, Arthur Jones rode home pursued by Roundheads. For thirty miles of rough country they were in hot pursuit, some reports stating that he had been mistaken as Charles II. Jones stabled his fatigued horse and came upstairs to eat. Before he could finish his meal, Cromwell's men had arrived. Jones's wife quickly secreted him in the hidden chamber. However, the good lady who had wined and dined the Roundheads so well was dismayed when they decided to stay the night. All was not lost; Jones's wife had seen fit to drug the copious amounts of wine they had drunk. While they slept, Jones made his getaway, complete with the Commander's horse.

Chastleton House, where Arthur Jones hid from Cromwell's soldiers in 1651.

CHIPPING NORTON

The Bliss & Son's tweed mill in Chipping Norton is a delightful piece of architecture which should now be classified as a folly as it has not served its original function since 1928. Designed by George Woodhouse in French chateaux style, the building boasts balustered parapets embellished by graceful urns. Far from the industrialised aspects of Lancashire towns, probably Woodhouse, a Lancastrian himself, decided to keep the building in tone with the rural countryside. However, all is somewhat spoilt by the massive Tuscan chimney.

Incidentally, a pub on the outskirts of Chipping Norton called the Quiet Woman once depicted a headless person on its sign.

Born in Chipping Norton in 1618, James Hind, the son of a saddler, received a surprisingly good education. Showing great courage in the Civil War, James was commissioned and made Captain Hind. Unfortunately, he had chosen the wrong side. The Royalists lost, the King was executed and Hind was out of a job. He then threw himself in with a notorious highwayman by the name of Thomas Allen. As a type of revenge for the King's death these two, along with several other gentlemen, attempted to ambush Cromwell's coach. The coach was well guarded and the ill-thought-out attack was a disaster. Hind escaped but Allen was arrested and executed.

Bliss Mill at Chipping Norton. (Author's collection)

By this time Hind was a much-wanted man and a full-blown highwayman, but as he was also successful and courteous, this made him popular with the public.

James Hind was a dyed in the wool Royalist, so when there was an attempt to put young Prince Charles on the throne, he offered his service. The attempt was doomed to failure. After the defeat at Worcester, Charles fled to his famous oak tree and then to France. Hind fled to London where he was arrested on criminal charges and lodged in Newgate. A charge of highway robbery was dropped due to insufficient evidence. A second charge of manslaughter stuck and James was sentenced to death, only to receive a pardon. The death penalty was reserved for those who had committed high treason. His enemies, however, would not give up. Hind was transported to Worcester where anti-Royalist feeling was at its highest. There he was convicted of treason and in the autumn of 1652, this adventurous and charismatic son of Chipping Norton was hanged, drawn and quartered.

CLAYDON

Claydon is situated on the most northern hilltop in the county where three stones stood in a field as the boundary of three counties. The villagers are justly proud of their old faceless clock which first rang 350 years ago. What it lacked in facial expression is more than compensated for with its lusty tongue.

Living nearly next door to the clock house was the village smithy where the admiring blacksmith's boy could hear the internal mechanics working. Unfortunately, the friendly old clock stopped and its tongue was stilled for a decade. Finally, the smith found time to venture into the belfry where he found a broken cog and peg. Being more used to the shoeing of horses and the mending of cartwheels and plough shares, the smith was very reticent to interfere with the intricate internal workings. But in 1940, he developed a metal ring that would hold the broken pieces together. The old bell rang out merrily throughout the Second World War and I presume it still does.

CROPREDY

Charles Stuart won one of the victories that led him into a false sense of achievement. Cannon-balls used in the battle were once displayed on a windowsill of the old church.

The chief treasure of the church is a solid brass lectern which displays a globe on which a glittering eagle stands. During the Civil War, this bird, accompanied by fifty others around the country, took flight and was successfully hidden. The lectern has three chubby little lions. After the war, the lectern, complete with globe, eagle and lions was resurrected from its hiding place deep in the River Cherwell. This task was not accomplished without unforeseen problems. The lectern had worked its way into the sludgy mud of the river bed. With much hard labour and with a crowbar and hoist, it slowly came to the surface. Sadly, one of the lions was missing, never to resurface. Instead, a local craftsman made a substitute from bronze. Unbeknown to the craftsman, the originals had been made of brass, a metal that was not easily be discerned in their dilapidated state. When they were finally cleaned and polished, the village discovered that the triplets were different colours, two blondes and a brunette.

DEDDINGTON

Deddington is a warm and friendly little village where one would expect to find a kindly and amiable ghost – and one would not be disappointed.

Maurice Frost was vicar of the parish until his death in 1962. Reputedly, his spirit returns to his old home to make sure his cherished books and his collection of antique clocks are being well cared for. However, this benign spirit is making fewer appearances as time passes by. He has been seen by several people, including his cousin who became quite accustomed to the spirits visitations and view his departure with regret.

'Drunken Deddington'. (Author's collection)

'Drunken Deddington' straddles the Oxford to Banbury Road, with a nickname that few of its citizens would be appreciative of today and which came about in a rather strange way. Deddington is justly proud of its church today but it is the church that unwittingly caused the reputation. The earlier tower collapsed in 1635 and the bells were left unguarded on the ground. Not neglecting a chance of profit, the villagers seized the bells and sold them to the army to make cannon-balls. The ecclesiastical authorities were not amused but the publicans were; what followed were a couple of months of drunken revelry.

FRITWELL

The grey stone manor of Fritwell is attractive but not conducive with longevity. In 1665, its owner was killed in a duel by a man named Pope Danvers. Danvers was arrested, tried, convicted and sentenced to death. For some reason, the execution was never carried out and soon after he walked free.

There is a story shortly afterwards about two brothers at Fritwell who loved the same lady. The facts are very flimsy and hard to discover but there are rumours of murder, suicide and skulduggery to the extreme.

Even later, a more verifiable story relates to the owner, Sir Baldwin Wake who was playing cards with his two sons. Accusing one of them of cheating, Sir Baldwin struck a blow that unfortunately proved fatal. This left Sir Baldwin a broken man; he had killed his first born and heir. To save his father from the authorities and public outcry, the younger son disappeared, taking the suspicion of murder with him. The truth was revealed twelve years later when Sir Baldwin, on his deathbed, admitted the truth. Fritwell Manor was not a lucky place; somewhere where one would have thought would be a fertile venue for ghosts, but try as I might, I have been unable to discover any evidence of one.

HARDWICK

There are traces here of a lost manor. The medieval oak granary complete with dovecot still exists, supported on rough-hewn stone piles. There is a lake covering eight acres which is responsible for a rather strange little story. In Queen Elizabeth I's golden days, a fugitive Jesuit priest donned the clothes of a labourer, excavated the lake, and worked in the gardens here for twelve years without being discovered. His only co-worker was a local man who knew the priest's story but was never tempted to inform on him.

There is a balustraded stone bridge that crosses part of the lake and in 1770, a Temple of Peace was erected by the owners, the Fermors, to their close friend, Alexander Pope.

HOOK NORTON

This attractive little village is famous nationwide for its brewery. I've enjoyed many a 'Little Hooky' myself. Less famous, but still worthy of mention is the font at the massive St Peter's Church. Along with the figures of Adam and Eve are strange carvings reputed to represent signs of the zodiac, though most experts think this is doubtful. The only figure that seems recognisable is an archer built like a centaur with the name Sagittarius printed beneath.

THE ROLLRIGHT STONES

This is an enchantingly eerie, if not scary place, situated on the A34, three miles north-west of Chipping Norton. If you catch it in the morning mist, as I have on several occasions, you'll know what I mean. There are actually three sites here, the story being that they were once a king and his troops. A large single stone represents the king, a group of five large stones, once a burial chamber, are the whispering knights and the numerous smaller stones, the army. There are countless strange stories here so I must be brief in my telling.

We are told that a king (which one is never mentioned) was trying to make all England his realm. He was marching towards Long Compton, a nearby ancient village, which even in those days had more witches than you could shake a stick at. As the king surmounted the hill, he met a witch. In a piece of (terrible) poetry, the witch informed the unnamed king that if he could take five steps and see Long Compton, he would shortly be king of all England. The king assumes this to be a simple task and takes the five steps. But unbeknown to him, there was a natural hill known as Archdruids Barrow blocking his view. For his failure, he and his troops were turned to stone.

There is another tale of a Long Compton baker who was told in a dream that if he counted the stones in the King's army, his business would be a success. The stones were actually said to be uncountable but the baker was crafty; he placed a loaf on every stone he counted. However, he was unsuccessful, as every time he looked around, one had gone missing.

Another story tells us of a vast stone, probably part of a burial chamber, being dragged down the hill to make a bridge. This seems to have been a pointless exercise as each day that it was dragged down, the following night it had spirited itself back up again. Incidentally, the King's Stone is reputed to take an occasional walk at night to drink at a nearby stream.

Witch ceremonies have been enacted for years at the Rollright Stones. They are often held in silence so as not to disturb the fairies that live there. One good witch sorted out the old hag that had turned the king to stone by turning her into an elder tree. When it was subsequently cut down, there was witches' blood in profusion.

The Rollright Stones.

The rocks also have other features. Some people have thought them to be lucky. Soldiers broke off chunks before going into battle, as apparently, the possession of slivers of rock made them invulnerable. Also, barren women walked around the rocks a certain number of times to cure their condition. Festivals of all types were celebrated at the Rollright Stones, and even today, people study them with scientific precision. Followers of ley lines and those that believe ancient circles contain a physical power have a specific interest.

While in the area in Long Sutton, there is a field where one can make a pact with the Devil. But be careful as you leave the Rollrights: A coach and horses lost control on the very steep gradient and its spectre still haunts the hill.

SANDFORD ST MARTIN

There is a grass mound that seems to be covering a small tunnel in the churchyard at Sandford St Martin which contains the coffin of Lord Deloraine, the third son of James, Duke of Monmouth. Lord Deloraine was but a boy of nine when his father met a tragic death. After the Battle of Sedgemoor, his defeated father was discovered hiding in a ditch. He was taken to Tower Hill and executed. However, Lord Deloraine later made a splendid career at the English court.

SHIRBURN

Shirburn is one of the county's prettiest villages. There is a splendid park here boasting a church and a castle. The church is easily visible but the remains of the castle are a little more difficult to discern as they are often covered by greenery. Shirburn has a massive round tower with a deep moat which has three bridges, one of which is guarded by a portcullis. Some of the stones date from the fourteenth century and Shirburn has been given as a prime example of a fortified house. Inside, there are several well-known works of art including *Erasmus* by Holbein and a picture of Catherine Parr with a lucky lock of hair in the frame. It must have worked as she was the only one of Henry VIII's fine ladies to survive. There is also a picture of Archbishop Laud by Van Dyke, who wasn't quite so lucky.

Here we also had a couple of self-made astronomers. Coming from the lowly station of stable boy, Thomas Phelps was to become one of the first men to note the 'Great Comet' and to have his observations noted by the Royal Society. Phelps was helped throughout by another notable astronomer, John Bartlett, a local shepherd. Between them, the shepherd and the stable boy became the most respected of British star-gazers. Phelps and Bartlett were helped from obscurity to distinction by the patronage of the Earl of Macclesfield, himself a notable astronomer, and it is chiefly owing to the influence he wielded that in 1752, a new calendar was initiated, eleven days shorter than the previous one. When the Bill was passed, a mob surrounded Parliament shouting, 'Give us back our eleven days!'

SOMERTON

To this day, we know little about the origins of a maze situated here called Troytown. Troytown is the name for literally dozens of mazes scattered all over Europe. Whether or not these have anything to do with the beautiful Helen and the besieged city is not known. Scholars differ on the subject and if there is a connection, it is a very tenuous one indeed. We know that the Troygame is played annually in Rome and had some religious significance, but the meaning is obscure and is sparingly reported. The maze at Somerton is well maintained but private. Its regular path is 400yds long but its age is totally unknown.

SOULDERN

The village of Souldern has a very well-authenticated ghost story, albeit back in 1706. The Revd Mr Shaw, the rector of Souldern and fellow of St John's College Cambridge, was in his library relaxing. He was somewhat surprised to have a visit from a friend, a Mr Naylor who had died some five years earlier.

The ghost pulled a chair over and they sat there chatting for an hour and a half. Where Mr Shaw inquired of his unexpected spook how things were 'beyond', Mr Naylor replied cheerfully that all was well but he missed his old college friends;

however, they would soon be with him. He said that Mr Arthur Orchard, known to them both, was on his way and that he, Mr Shaw would be following shortly. How true Naylor's prediction was is not known, but no doubt the reverend was more than a little worried.

STEEPLE ASHTON

Steeple Ashton straddles the Oxford to Banbury road. Years ago, this route was a favourite of road agents, footpads and highwaymen. These were usually brutal bullies of the Dick Turpin ilk but Steeple Ashton, where the Hopcrofts Holt stands, is reputed to have been the preferred domain of Claude Duval. Duval, a Frenchman, came to England in the service of gentlemen and it is from them that he learnt his courteous manners. One of the many stories of Duval tells how he would let a wealthy coach passenger retain half his money if he would dance with his lovely daughter. In all probability, this is a true report unlike anything heard about Turpin. Hopcroft was the name of a local innkeeper who was in cahoots with Claude Duval and often hid him from pursuing posses.

The Hopcroft Holt today still has a well-carved sign depicting a highwayman complete with French coach, doeskin breeches and tricorn hat. At the back of the sign stands a gallows, possibly a grim reminder of the fate of Duval who met his maker at Tyburn in 1670. He was 27 years old. If the handsome, rascally Frenchman did frequent the Hopcrofts Holt, and there seems little doubt that he did, then in all probability, it was a previous building on the same site. The present inn was constructed in 1734, some time after Duval's death.

UPPER HEYFORD

This is air force country, but the only thing of strange and ancient interest is known as Aves Ditch, which is actually a great earth wall, just over a mile long. This Wansdyke-like construction would seem to have little justification for its existence. A vestige of Aves Ditch can be traced from Roman Akeman Street where it crosses the Cherwell, near Kirkington, a large Saxon settlement, to Souldern on the Northamptonshire border some six miles away. There is a school of thought that maintains that Ades Ditch is a remnant of a far greater West Saxon construction that was built to separate them from Mercia. Another opinion is that it was built by the Romans as a defence for Akeman Street.

The Holt Hotel inn sign, Steeple Ashton, on the site of what was once a haunt of highwaymen. (Author's collection)